Simon Jenkins is a journalist and author. He writes for the *Guardian* as well as broadcasting for the BBC. He was political editor of *The Economist* and has written for and edited *The Times* and the *London Evening Standard*. His books include *A Short History of England* and *The Battle for the Falklands* (co-authored by Max Hastings). He has also written on architecture and chaired the National Trust.

'As I expected, I found Simon's book sharply observed, excellently judged, and pretty much unanswerable. His arguments are crystal-clear, and often savage. Highly readable, informed by Jenkins' own observations from the ground, this is a book of remarkable precision and intelligence. I just hope that everyone who argued in favour of the various interventions he writes about will have the decency to read it, and repent; but I don't suppose for a moment that most of them will.'

JOHN SIMPSON

'A rare and intriguing voyage. Most of us would not dare to do what Simon Jenkins has done – revisit what he wrote on issues which are still current. Too often journalists turn out to be right in their reporting, and the decision makers prove to be wrong. Here's a book that proves it.'

JON SNOW

MISSION ACCOMPLISHED?

THE CRISIS OF INTERNATIONAL INTERVENTION

SIMON JENKINS

I.B. TAURIS

LONDON · NEW YORK

Published in paperback in 2015 by
I.B.Tauris & Co. Ltd
London • New York
www.ibtauris.com

References to websites were correct at the time of writing.

ISBN: 978 1 78453 132 4
eISBN: 978 0 85773 917 9

A full CIP record for this book is available from the British Library
A full CIP record is available from the Library of Congress

Library of Congress Catalog Card Number: available

Typeset in Goudy by OKS Prepress Services, Chennai, India
Printed and bound by Page Bros, Norwich

Contents

Preface

The end of the Cold War with the Soviet Union left Western governments seeking a new sense of purpose on the world stage. They found it in the profession of the policeman. They concerned themselves with countries that had, in their view, offended international peace and order and also standards of good behaviour towards their own peoples. This intervention moved from that of charitable aid and exhortation to economic sanction and eventually military aggression. The turn of the twenty-first century has come to be known as the age of intervention – humanitarian, liberal, neo-conservative or neo-imperial according to taste. The targets were almost all small Muslim states.

By 2015 sheer exhaustion – and a public perception of failure – appeared to be bringing this age to an end. At any rate a definable period in international relations appeared to have reached punctuation. This book is not a history of that period or an essay on military intervention. It is a commentary on events as I saw them at the time, commentary in context.

I was sceptical of most, though not all, of these wars, puzzled by the urge of Western democracies to return to the battlefield after decades in which their statesmen had meticulously avoided it. In particular I was surprised at younger people finding nothing exceptional in unprovoked aggression against foreign states or in their armed forces bombing civilian populations. These were, after all, "wars of choice" not of self-defence. Few were set-piece battles, rather what strategists call "wars among the people" on foreign soil. As such they were hard to explain and hard to "win". Yet apart from Iraq in 2003 they encountered little public opposition.

Almost all wars are reported from one side or the other, from that of the bomber or the bombed. During the period covered in this book,

I visited most of the places in contention, including Serbia, Iraq, Afghanistan, Pakistan, the Gulf, Lebanon and Syria, plus frequent trips to America. That said, I am not a foreign correspondent let alone a war reporter. My beat is mostly London. Wars of intervention arise in large part from the political climate in the intervening states, in this case America and Britain. Action is determined by decisions in their capitals, driven by domestic pressures on leaders, by alliances, military traditions, public opinion and the media.

During this time I was writing some 1,200 words of commentary for various British newspapers, usually twice a week. Revisiting such material after the event may seem self-indulgent, but I hope that retelling recent history through contemporary witness might help it to seem fresh. I was intrigued to see where I was right or wrong, how far my judgments stood the test of time. I harbour no pretence that what commentators write influences events, but it does feed into political debate. As such, its validity matters. It cannot be bad for writers on current affairs sometimes to consider their words in the light of history. They might proceed with greater caution next time.

The extracted material appeared from 1999 to 2014 in the *London Times* and the *Guardian*. None of the words have been changed, though most entries have been shortened to avoid repetition. None have been "censored" to save authorial embarrassment. Where I was wrong, and I reflect on this at the end, I can only say I believed it at the time.

Simon Jenkins

Introduction

In the summer of 1992 I was invited for a briefing to the private office of the British foreign secretary, Douglas Hurd. The room overlooking St James's Park was festooned with pictures and paraphernalia recalling the British Empire, its triumphs and its ruling personalities. From this room for centuries, edicts had gone out setting the world to rights. It was perhaps not the best place to give a sense of proportion to Britain's diminished role overseas. Hurd was struggling to do just that.

The former communist state of Yugoslavia was decomposing. While the separation of Slovenia in 1991 had passed peacefully to independence, that of Croatia a year later was fiercely resisted by the Yugoslav government in Belgrade, and by the province's Serb population. The result was a bitter civil war, awash in atrocities on both sides. The Germans were supporting the Croats. Most other countries, including America, were in favour of neutrality, a so-called "level playing field". Either way, humanitarian relief was urgently needed. This Britain was supplying but there was a dispute over military protection for the relief convoys.

Hurd was dog-tired and kept nodding off during the conversation. But he was adamant to convey one message, that the "rules of engagement" for the escorts were to avoid contact and fire only in self-defence. There would be no "mission creep". However terrible the conflict, said Hurd, it was not Britain's business. For good measure, Washington's military chief, General Colin Powell, said the same. Britain was in Red Cross mode, intervening impartially to relieve all those suffering in war.

Hurd was honouring a long-standing principle of the UN, set out in the Charter's Chapter I, Article 2. This states, "All Members shall refrain in their international relations from the threat or use of force against the territorial integrity or political independence of any state … Nothing contained in the present Charter shall authorize the United Nations to intervene in matters which are essentially within the domestic jurisdiction of any state." This assertion of sovereign integrity is traced back to the 1648 Peace of Westphalia. In the UN's case, in the aftermath of World War II, it underpinned the willingness to join the UN of many non-democratic states, notably within the communist bloc. Without it there would have been no such world body.

The article was moderated, some might say undermined, by the subsequent Chapter VII, referring to state actions that breached "international peace and security". In such cases the UN authorised itself to take enforcement measures to restore such peace, but the crucial qualifier was "international peace". Again this was regarded as vital to ensure the assent of nations that might regard their own internal peace as a matter for them. Thus the stress remained on respecting state sovereignty and territorial integrity.

The history of the UN has long seen pious intention corrupted by realpolitik. Chapter I was largely disregarded by "spheres of influence", the alliances and "unequal treaties" of the Cold War. There was an acceptance that Washington might intervene at will in South America, as might Moscow along the borders of the Warsaw Pact. The Charter was always vulnerable to the geo-strategic interests of the great powers. The price was paid by Hungary and Czechoslovakia, and by Guatemala and Chile.

My own witness to such interventions began somewhere else, in the final years of the Vietnam War in 1973. It was an eerie time to visit Saigon. The American army had left but the South Vietnamese regime had not yet collapsed. The city's artillery defences against the advancing Vietcong could be heard at night, booming across the countryside. No one could quite believe Saigon itself would fall and Japanese speculators were buying abandoned properties across the city. Yet the bars and briefing rooms reeked with impending doom. A terrible mistake was coming to an unthinkable end. America was about to be beaten.

This was a war from which Britain stood aloof. Yet under the UN Charter's Chapter VII it was not unjustified. South Vietnam was subject to blatant aggression from the north and activated its alliance with America to protect its sovereignty. Communist China was pursuing a patently aggressive "domino" expansion through south-east Asia, threatening Laos, Cambodia, Thailand and possibly Indonesia. Australia sent troops to Vietnam on that basis.

The war was conducted by Washington with astonishing incompetence. Its belief in the efficacy of air power alienated potentially friendly buffer territories, conceding Laos, Cambodia and finally all of Vietnam to communism. It was a warning to any power, however great, that military might alone is neither a necessary nor a sufficient condition for victorious intervention overseas.

The same was later true of successive interventions, economic, diplomatic and rhetorical. In Lebanon in the 1970s and 1980s, UN forces led by America arrived to separate the feuding factions and failed. Only a Syrian invasion established peace. A barrage of Western abuse of Cuba, Libya, Burma, North Korea and Iran was followed by often savage economic sanctions. They did not topple but rather cemented targeted regimes in power, often for long periods of time.

The UN Charter was respected more assiduously elsewhere, perhaps where Western interests were less at stake. There was a notable reluctance to engage in sub-Saharan Africa. The civil war in Ethiopia in 1983–5 saw thousands die as famine was used as a weapon of oppression by the government. World response was limited to humanitarian relief. The same applied to civil wars in Uganda, Rwanda and Congo. In south-east Asia, the brutal regime of Pol Pot in Cambodia in the 1980s evoked condemnation but little else, despite the deaths of between 1 and 3 million people.

With the end of the Cold War, opinion began to shift. While the Soviet sphere of influence lost its potency, the West's triumph heralded new opportunities and obligations. In 1991 the UN secretary-general, Javier Perez de Cuellar, gave what appeared to be a death sentence in Chapter I: "We are clearly witnessing what is probably an irresistible shift in public attitudes toward the belief that the defence of the oppressed in the name of morality should prevail over frontiers and legal documents."

Over the following decade this view was gradually fashioned into a doctrine that governments had a "responsibility to protect" their people from "genocide, war crimes, crimes against humanity and ethnic cleansing". Increasing references were made to past wars against dictatorship, to the Nuremburg concept of "crimes against humanity". By implication this imposed on the international community an obligation to sanction states failing in that responsibility. So-called R2P asserted that if a country ignored certain norms of behaviour, its sovereignty could be overridden, at least by the UN. The door to the age of interventionism lay ajar.

The first post-Cold War intervention was the 1991 Gulf War to liberate Kuwait from an Iraqi invasion. The action was approved by the UN and fell clearly within the terms of Chapter VII. It was a success, scrupulously respecting UN principles in spirit and letter by refusing to pursue Iraqi forces from Kuwait across Iraq to Baghdad. Once defeated, Saddam was left in power – a decision later described by Washington hawks as "unfinished business".

For America, Kuwait laid the ghost of Vietnam. General Colin Powell's doctrine of overwhelming force had worked where diplomatic persuasion failed. Soon afterwards, in December 1992, an emboldened Washington plunged into the civil war in Somalia, sending 25,000 troops ashore, again under UN auspices, with guns blazing. The action was ill-planned and disastrous. Eight months later the marines retreated from a chaotic Mogadishu, a defeat later recorded in the film, *Black Hawk Down*.

The reaction to Somalia was a minor echo of Vietnam. It conditioned an American refusal the following year to intervene to halt the Rwandan massacre, when almost a million people met their deaths, despite clear warnings in the world's press. What was lacking was any guiding principle to such interventions. Ideological struggle had been replaced by international justice (in Kuwait) and humanitarianism (in Somalia). But these were vague concepts, subject to variable interpretation, confusion and not a little hypocrisy.

In 1992 the veteran statesman of Vietnam, Henry Kissinger, warned against the mission creep to which humanitarian intervention was vulnerable, especially where it meant involvement in other people's civil wars. He worried at Americans thinking "that moral and humane concerns are so much a part of American life that not only treasure but lives must be risked to vindicate them".[1]

Where, asked Kissinger, would this stop? It implied that America had an obligation, a covenant, a manifest destiny not just to set an example to the world but to impose that example on others. No other nation, said Kissinger (perhaps forgetting Britain), "has ever put forward such a set of propositions". Indeed such intervention invited "a rogue nation to use the slogan for its own expansionist designs".

Yet the concept was becoming embedded in the public conscience. The *Washington Post* declared at the time of Somalia that "in just a few years the idea has been established that countries that fail to care decently for their citizens dilute their claim to sovereignty and forfeit invulnerability to outside political-military intervention".[2]

When the disintegration of Yugoslavia spread to Bosnia later in 1992, the resulting atrocities still did not stimulate foreign involvement. Evidence of thousands slaughtered or interned in concentration camps led to the arrival of UN "peace-keepers" but they were of startling ineffectiveness. Not until the Srebrenica massacre and the 1995 siege of Sarajevo did world opinion snap. This led the UN to authorise tactical air strikes by NATO against the Serb besiegers of Sarajevo. These strikes, coupled with reverses in the war with Croatia, eventually drove the Serb leader, Slobodan Milošević, to back down and agree the so-called Dayton Accords.

At the time, the American president Bill Clinton was told that congressional support for sending American troops to Yugoslavia was "virtually zero". Somalia was a lesson learned. America might offer the good offices (and bombers) of a great power, but its soldiers would not be sent round the world to die for someone else's cause. America's role was not "about fighting a war" but about helping the sides reach a peace. The US national security adviser at the time, Anthony Lake, added that it was "dangerous hubris" to think America could rebuild nations. It could merely "help nations build themselves".

---

[1]   *International Herald Tribune* 12.14.1992.

[2]   *International Herald Tribune* 27.11.1992.

Bosnia and Dayton, coming on the heels of Rwanda, were a crucial spur to the cause of what came to be defined as liberal interventionism. A careful account by a Harvard analyst working in Bosnia at the time, Gerald Knaus, emphasised the limited contribution of NATO's intervention to its resolution.[3] He said that "claims that US planes bombed recalcitrant Bosnian Serbs into accepting a peace deal are misleading". The success of the Bosnian intervention was in large part due to timing, not much-publicised bombing. The attacking Serbs were exhausted. Tactical bombing of their bases added to the pressure. But settlement resulted essentially from a shifting reality on the ground.

The resulting Dayton agreement of November 1995 was the work of the experienced US diplomat, Richard Holbrooke. He carefully assessed the personalities, weaknesses and territorial dispositions of the different groups. The country contained just 4 million people (smaller than Wales) and was divided into three essentially autonomous sectors. Money was hurled at its administration, infrastructure and public services. Bosnians became the most subsidised people on earth.

Despite initial reservations, 20,000 American troops were sent to Bosnia as part of a foreign peacekeeping force of over 60,000. It was to be the highest ratio of peacekeepers to population in the entire age of intervention, some 20 to each 1,000 of the population in the contested areas. It compared with Somalia's five to each thousand and Afghanistan's four.[4]

Nonetheless, the Bosnian intervention was essentially a triumph not for war but for, highly delayed, diplomatic intervention.[5] It restored law and order, captured war criminals and secured the return of evicted peoples to their former villages. It was greatly facilitated by the fact that the war was over when they arrived. They suffered not a single casualty. Bosnia was also a European nation. It was governed by an EU high representative with no date for

---

[3] Knaus with Rory Stewart, *Can Intervention Work?*, 2011.

[4] Knaus, p. 132.

[5] Owen, *Balkan Odyssey*, 1995.

withdrawal. Bosnia became (and remains) in effect an EU colony, the first of the new age.

Bosnia changed the terms of the debate. It became the "good intervention", the starting point for the age of intervention and "nation building" from Kosovo to Sierra Leone, Afghanistan, Iraq and Lebanon. After Bosnia, says Knaus, "it became commonplace to refer to all these missions as if they were variations on the same theme". A universalist template was placed over every atrocity or conflict. Intervention had worked in Bosnia. Its day was at hand.

A new challenge soon emerged. In December 1998, Iraq returned to centre stage with wrangles over its non-compliance with UN weapons inspection. Tony Blair joined President Clinton in Operation Desert Fox, an aerial attack on targets in Iraq to eliminate Saddam Hussein's "weapons of mass destruction". A more urgent motive for the campaign appeared to be to distract domestic American attention from Clinton's Monica Lewinsky scandal then obsessing Washington. The weapons were afterwards said to have been "degraded" – a claim impossible to verify – but the no-fly zone along the Kurdistan border did effectively prevent military operations by Saddam against the Kurds.

Bosnia and Desert Fox broke a stalemate that had gripped the overseas power projection of the Western nations since Somalia in 1992. They offered a sort of answer not just to various threats to international order, real or imagined, but to any sort of humanitarian evil that flashed across the world's television screens. Where there was ever greater access to news and thus an ever more heightened susceptibility to "concern", intervention was what the cliché of the age most craved, evidence that "something can be done". People were not condemned to the moral exhaustion of "sitting idly by" and "just doing nothing". The guilt of Rwanda could be atoned.

As we shall see over its course, the age of intervention was ideologically confused. Ostensibly it presented a Greek narrative of *hamartia* (or mistake) followed by hubris and nemesis. Or it could be seen as a dialectic of thesis (Bosnia), antithesis (Iraq) and synthesis (Syria/Islamic State). These parallels can be applied according to taste. But at intervention's heart lay a simple clash of motives, a clash that became the jangling chorus of the age, a cacophony of twisted logic, shifting premises and sheer mendacity.

To some (mostly on the right) intervention was a tool of national security and world order. It was essentially defensive. This involved a series of claims, much beloved of George Bush and Tony Blair, whereby national security required the suppression of "terror states", the export of democratic institutions and the establishment of world order. In the initial attacks on Afghanistan and Iraq, Bush constantly stated that they were vital to America's security.

Before the Iraq invasion, in June 2003, Bush told a West Point audience that he now rejected the "Cold War doctrines of deterrence and containment". America, if necessary alone, would "take the battle to the enemy, disrupt his plans and confront the worst threats before they emerge". He claimed the right to pre-emptive aggression against any state that might threaten America, or its neighbours, or even its own people.

The British government likewise justified the Iraq invasion by virtue of Iraq's "clear and present threat" to Britain, indeed a 45-minute threat. Nor was it just terrorism. As Blair was to say of intervention in general, "We cannot turn our backs on conflicts and the violation of human rights within other countries if we want to stay secure."[6]

At no point in this period was America, Britain or any other Western power threatened territorially or economically by the targeted states. The West faced terrorist attacks, some of them dreadful, but these did not undermine any state's national security, properly so called. The nations of NATO had never been less threatened or more safe in their history. The concept of intervention for pre-emptive national security was little more than an assertion of might is right and has nothing else to do.

That is perhaps why, as the age evolved, intervention to defend national security elided into, and indeed hijacked, the quite different liberal argument, that intervention was humanitarian. It was to save lives and promote values. Thus Bush, who said he went to war with Iraq to protect America and suppress terrorism, could claim a quite different objective when he declared afterwards that his mission was

---

[6] Chicago speech, April 1999.

"accomplished". He told his audience on a Gulf warship that the battle had been fought "for the cause of liberty and for the peace of the world . . . the tyrant has fallen and Iraq is free".

Again these motives too were mixed. The actual saving of lives was a long-standing reason for intervention, even before responsibility to protect. It had the virtue of being specific and limited, and in the short term hard to protest. Only as it broadened and lengthened did it become confused with a more general interventionism. But then every warrior sees himself as "saving lives". As for "promoting values", what did that mean? We would all like to see a world in which democracy, human rights, public welfare and freedom of speech can flourish. But to convert this into a specific *casus belli* takes some argument.

In the first place it is hopelessly vulnerable to the charge of hypocrisy. We seem concerned for human rights where it suits our interests – in some parts of the Muslim world – but not in others. We supported the Taliban when they were against the Russians. We supported Saddam Hussein when he was against Iran. We ignore repression in Saudi Arabia and China. The age of intervention almost completely neglected sub-Saharan Africa, scene of the worst human atrocities that took place during the age of intervention: of all the charges that might be laid against the age, that of blatant racism is hardest to resist.

In his succinct dissection of "the dangers and delusions" of liberal interventionism, Roger Howard took apart these vague objectives and showed each to be meaningless.[7] "What we really mean when we talk about human rights", he said, "is that at any given moment particular people are placing particular value upon particular interests."

Indeed Howard sees darker motives in the liberal's enthusiasm for intervention. It recaptures John Stuart Mill's preaching of the "civilising imperialism" of the West. It recaptures America's Cold War adventurism, notably in Latin America. Is it any wonder, asks Howard, that liberal humanitarianism "has become fashionable at the same time as old-fashioned socialism has fallen into disrepute,

---

[7] Howard, *What's Wrong with Liberal Interventionism*, 2006.

as if the visions of creating 'heaven on earth' have crumbled at home and been refocused abroad?" Likewise Bush and the American neo-conservatives seem anything but conservative. Their global ambition in seeking to bring about the overthrow of Islamic "values" can only be seen as "deeply un-conservative, inherently flawed and ultimately doomed".

This confusion of motives was a leitmotif of the age of intervention. It drew to its banner a huge but motley army of statesmen, soldiers, diplomats, security consultants, charity workers, arms dealers, aid thieves and crooks. Its staggering expenditure may have impoverished millions but it enriched thousands. The bursting bank vaults of Amman and Beirut, the gleaming towers and empty villas of Dubai, are its most visible memorials.

I now take up the narrative. The interventions in Bosnia and Desert Fox had not put in place a framework of deterrence that might forestall future evils. In Serbia, Milošević remained in power but was threatened by another province in his shrinking domain. Kosovo's "liberation army" (KLA) had long been black listed by Washington as a terrorist organisation. But when in mid-1998 the KLA led an armed uprising against its Serbian rulers, its status shifted to that of plucky separatist.

In June 1998, in a foretaste of things to come, Clinton declared the conflict in Kosovo an American "national emergency" due to an "unusual and extraordinary threat to the national security and foreign policy of the United States". This was patent nonsense. But despite the absence of UN authority, NATO prepared bombing targets in Serbia, commencing a game of bluff and double-bluff that continued into the following spring. This had the effect of stimulating a devastating "ethnic cleansing" of Kosovan Albanians, the Serb army driving them from their homes over the border into Macedonia. Tales of atrocities poured out of Kosovo, culminating in January 1999 in the massacre of some 45 villagers by Serb forces in the village of Racak.

Throughout this period British politicians, driven by the media, were gazing in despair at the unfolding tragedy. Surely something "must be done", but what?

1

Into Yugoslavia

Over the course of 1998 British ministers had spent weeks deploring the Serb leader, Slobodan Milošević, for constantly agreeing to withdraw his troops from Kosovo, where they were imposing appalling oppression and ethnic cleansing on the local population, and then not doing so. The Racak massacre of January 1999 was the last straw. What could Britain do? What more could the foreign secretary, Robin Cook, say? In the House of Commons he could only denounce Milošević and his actions as "deeply foolish ... unacceptable ... shocking ... murderous ... horrific". [House of Commons, 18/19.01.1999]

29.01.1999

MR COOK recites all this with sombre mien. He then looks down at his word list and finds the armoury is bare. His mouth opens and shuts in silence. There is just a ghost whispering in his ear, "Real men drop bombs." We are back to our old friend, the bomb. British foreign policy is now a four-letter word. So bankrupt is this neo-Palmerstonian stance, so counter-productive to its goals, so devoid of success, that it can only respond to 45 dead Albanians by threatening 45 dead Serbs. Policy is dumbed-down to a bomb for a bomb and a corpse for a corpse. Dictators who sneer at Mr Cook's heat-seeking adjectives must feel the blast of his heat-seeking bombs.

The reason for bombing Yugoslavia is to alter the balance of power on the ground in Kosovo. That is achieved only by sending in troops. Such invasion is what the KLA have been encouraged by Mr Cook's policy to expect. Is it meant? If not, the threat cruelly invites KLA resurgence and ruthless Serbian suppression. But invasion cannot police an active civil war. It must either assist the KLA in the military dismembering of a European state. Or it must help the Serbs to restore Yugoslav sovereignty against KLA rebellion. Which of these dreadful goals is now British policy?

Former Yugoslavia has seen every phase of "new world order" mission creep. First it welcomed humanitarian aid to civil war victims. Then it saw foreign governments drawn into protecting that aid with troops. The protection became partisan. Heavy weapons arrived. The troops became militarily active, then players in local politics.

The British people were categorically promised that Britain would not become embroiled in the war of Yugoslavia's succession. The promise has not been kept. The logic of intervention was inescapable from the arrival of the first humble soldier to the present computerised bomb-targeting of the whole of Yugoslavia. This is what historians call the madness of war.

Britain is currently also conducting a bombing campaign against Iraq in support of the War of Clinton's Frustration. It is mere bombing. Toppling Saddam Hussein would plainly require a ground assault and Britain has neither the will nor the guts for that. If Anglo-American forces invaded, against the opposition of half the world, they would have to fight and stay. As in Bosnia and presumably in Kosovo, they would have to take responsibility for the aftermath. They would need to be proper policemen, rather than the present hit-and-run vendetta squad.

The impasse over Kosovo continued into February amid mounting violence on the ground. This precipitated a conference at Rambouillet outside Paris and an "Accord" of March 1999. This collapsed on the refusal of Serbia to allow the stationing of NATO monitors on its soil. Milošević duly intensified his ethnic cleansing, until almost a million Albanians had been driven from Kosovo into Macedonia.

NATO now lost patience. On the night of 24 March it began bombing selective Serb targets. The attack was not authorised by the UN due to Russian opposition, and was technically illegal in international law. At the same time both Bill Clinton and Tony Blair specifically ruled out a ground invasion of Kosovo, confining themselves to moving troops to neighbouring Macedonia, supposedly to protect future ceasefire monitors. Intervention was to be left to the bombers.

24.03.1999

WHY KOSOVO? Why, of all the current civil wars and humanitarian horrors, is it Kosovo that now summons British troops to the colours? Or put it another way, why does a bloodstained shroud only have to wave over a Balkan village for otherwise intelligent people to take leave of their senses?

Yesterday the West tossed another gauntlet before the Yugoslav leader, Slobodan Milošević. All previous ultimatums have been bluffs, and he has called them. In response to a month of NATO sabre-rattling, he has unleashed on Kosovo a pre-emptive scorched-earth campaign of medieval brutality. Now squadrons of bombers are waiting to pulverise his country, and 10,000 NATO troops stand ready to invade from Macedonia. Yet a BBC interviewer yesterday could gasp "How can Milošević be so stupid?" A wise general never asks that question of his enemy, only of his friends.

In the early 1960s, Americans considered it unthinkable that a modern President such as John Kennedy could entangle the United States in a third land war in the Far East within 20 years. It was simply beyond imagining that, in a nuclear age, American boys would ever again die fighting in distant jungles. The world was too safe and Kennedy too shrewd and too liberal to make such a mistake. Besides, America was omnipotent. The orientals would be no match for the rolling thunder of the world's mightiest air force.

The historian Barbara Tuchman famously addressed the puzzle of Vietnam and concluded that, in the matter of war, little had changed since the fall of Troy. In *The March of Folly*, she related how each crisis was confounded by vain and hesitant leaders, by fears of retreat, by deafness to unpalatable advice and by a constant belief "that there was no choice". Kennedy had to take America into Vietnam to prove he was tough on communism, and Lyndon Johnson to prove that "I am not going to lose it". After half a million dead, it was lost. Nothing was gained, and it appears nothing was learnt.

I cannot find a single strategist to give me a level-headed outline of Britain's war aims in Yugoslavia. The objective set out by Mr Blair appears to be to bomb the Serbs into granting partial autonomy to Kosovo. It is scarcely credible that a serious person can believe this will be done by bombs – least of all after the Iraqi experience – and Mr Blair was unable to say how. The action seems certain both to kill more civilians and to provoke bloody retaliation against the Kosovans, which NATO is powerless to prevent. What kind of humanitarianism is that?

Last year the British government sent 3,000 troops as part of the 10,000 NATO force in Macedonia. They were to help get Western monitors out of Kosovo in the event of danger. Then they were to go in and "keep the peace" at the invitation of both sides. Now, according to one of their commanders, they are to "separate the combatants and disarm them", a feat that for 30 years defied the British Army in Northern Ireland. Next week, if Mr Blair is not cruelly deceiving the Kosovans, the objective may have to be to confront 40,000 Serb troops in open battle.

This is not so much mission creep as mission stampede. But if it happens, it does give point to the Opposition leader [William Hague's] question yesterday: why did NATO not act sooner before it allowed Mr Milošević to deploy his full army on its southern front facing NATO? If British troops are to die in the cause of Kosovan autonomy, this delay will seem criminally negligent.

The March bombing of military targets failed to induce Milošević to climb down in Kosovo. The targets were duly widened to include government buildings and infrastructure such as power lines, electricity generators and even the bridges over the Danube. This halted river traffic into the heart of Europe. The next targets were television stations and the Chinese embassy, allegedly because of a radio transmitter in its attic. After six weeks, Milošević's position hardened and his brutality in Kosovo increased.

In April 1999 Tony Blair, deeply frustrated by American indecision, travelled to America and gave a speech in Chicago in which he advocated a new humanitarian interventionism under a "doctrine of international community". This community would intervene militarily not in self-defence or self-interest but to save peoples from repressive governments. It was an echo of the ideology of the Edwardian imperialist, Alfred Milner, of a Britain with a manifest destiny to a moral or "constructive" empire. Blair laid down five preconditions for intervention: that "you" (unspecified) be sure of your case; you exhaust all other options; you ask if military operations can be "sensibly" undertaken; you be prepared for the long term; and you have identified your interests involved. I wondered which other countries and conflicts across the globe might be suitable targets.

05.05.1999

MR BLAIR addresses Albanian refugees with the cry, "This is not a battle for territory, this is a battle for humanity". We duly turn to the website of the United Nations High Commissioner for Refugees and its chilling checklist of man's inhumanity to man. An estimated 30 million people are currently clamouring to be the objects of Mr Blair's crusade. Sixteen million are in Africa, seven million in Asia, five million in Europe and three million in the Americas. The overwhelming majority have been driven from their homes, often at the point of a gun, by civil upheaval inside their own countries. At the top of this league table are two million Sudanese, followed by Angolans, Burmese, Bosnians, Rwandans, Iraqis, Armenians, Azeris, Chechens, Colombians and Eritreans.

Even in the ruthlessness of their eviction, Kosovans are well down the list. In each case, the cause of misery is political collapse. It is the failure of a nation state to maintain internal discipline while tolerating minority races, tribes or religious groups. Humankind cannot bear very much reality, said Eliot. But nor can it bear very much geography.

The now-defunct United Nations principle of non-interference in the internal affairs of states was not self-interested or cynical. It was merely clear. It permitted, indeed obliged, wars to restore the integrity of states, as in the Falklands and Kuwait. To Margaret Thatcher in 1983, it made America's invasion of Grenada wrong.

The conflicts that are currently involving outside powers in the civil rights of subordinate groups within states embrace Palestinians, Irish nationalists, Kurds and Kosovans. Such intervention cannot avoid altering the balance of power in these conflicts, but to what end? American support for the IRA over the years materially affected the

Ulster conflict, yet gave Mr Clinton no leverage over weapons decommissioning. Last winter's NATO saber-rattling against Belgrade emboldened the KLA to step up its terror campaign in Kosovo and the Serbs to promote ethnic cleansing. Were such opportunistic interventions successful as a means to peace, they might be applauded. They were not.

By June 1999 NATO (that is primarily America) faced international opposition to the apparently useless bombing of civilian targets, which included dropping free-fall explosives on civic buildings, and even market places in the cities, such as Novi Sad and Nis. Bombing was clearly not going to drive Serbia out of Kosovo, let alone topple Milošević.

Preparations were duly made for a ground invasion by NATO troops stationed in Macedonia. An ultimatum told Milošević to withdraw from Kosovo or face invasion. Serbia's hitherto ally, Russia, decided enough was enough and declined to back Milošević with fuel supplies. Moscow would not be taking sides against NATO in a ground war in Europe. The ultimatum worked.

04.06.1999

SLOBODAN MILOŠEVIĆ yesterday pulled his country back from a certain sort of brink. He also hauled NATO back from the ghastliness of embarking on a ground war in landlocked Europe. According to information from Belgrade, the catalyst was a specific threat delivered by Martti Ahtisaari from Bill Clinton. It was the one threat that NATO had so far declined to offer, not a continuation of bombing but an invasion of Kosovo in which America would be a full participant.

Winning support for that invasion had become a central objective of the British government and was thus a tactical triumph for Tony Blair. Had the same threat from NATO been made last March – rather than specifically denied by both Clinton and Blair – how much horror might have been avoided? Yesterday's events should not be regarded as a triumph for the "bombing alone" lobby. Quite the opposite.

History will see the Kosovan crisis as embracing two punitive expeditions, together leaving Kosovo an empty and wasted land. The first saw a reckless state, Serbia, its army dehumanised by years of civil war, reacting to separatist violence by driving a million people from their land by terror and the sword. The second saw Britain and America seeking to express their disapproval, but without pain to themselves.

The bombers left those on the ground thoroughly bombed, and those in the air feeling much better. Eventually push came to shove, but only when the means denied at the start were conceded at the end. War is still about fighting, not bombing.

The withdrawal of Serb forces led to the return of some 800,000 Albanian refugees and the establishment of a Western protectorate in Pristina, similar to that established under the 1995 Dayton Accords in Bosnia. As such, the Kosovo intervention was hailed a success for the new interventionism – and for Blair, its most ardent prophet. The previously "terrorist" KLA was installed in power. Yet in neither Bosnia nor Kosovo was a free-standing political regime established. Both remain under international protection and supervision to this day.

Three months after the June end of hostilities, military analysts met in Toronto to assess the outcome, amid conflicting claims for the efficacy of air versus land power. There was no denying the war objective had been achieved in the return of refugees and the eviction of Serb authority from Kosovo. But what really made Milošević capitulate? Was it an estimated 38,000 NATO air sorties, including many against civilian targets, or was it the threat of a land war?

24.09.1999

I DISTRUST strategic bombing and therefore suffer the same handicap as do its advocates. I tend to grasp at any evidence that supports my view, and dismiss what upsets it. But history is a stern tyrant. It orders us to leave prejudice at the gate before we enter.

The bombing of military and civilian targets in Yugoslavia continued throughout the Kosovo conflict, from 24 March to 9 June. The ferocity of the assault masked the fact that air power, first threatened then actual, did not deter Milošević in the slightest. It did not meet its professed goal of "halting ethnic cleansing in Kosovo", let alone "in a matter of days". Whether the bombing was catalyst to more atrocity than might have occurred had the foreign observers stayed in place is moot. What is certain is that the bombing did nothing to impede the cleansing, which could hardly have been worse.

By May, Pentagon and CIA officials were contradicting reports emanating from NATO headquarters in Brussels and from British ministers in the House of Commons. The bombing was assessed (in leaks to *The New York Times*) as having only "a marginal effect" on operations in Kosovo. Nor was there any sign of a change of heart in Belgrade. On 4 May, General Klaus Naumann, the chairman of NATO's military committee, publicly admitted that bombing had failed. The International Institute for Strategic Studies issued a report baffled at the tactical purpose of telling the Serbs that there would be no land invasion.

Recent briefing has revealed furious rows within NATO command at that time, notably between General Wesley Clark and his US Air Force chief, Michael Short. General Clark could not see why bombers were not hitting targets in Kosovo. General Short regarded such "tank-plinking" as a waste of time and money; rightly as it turned out. His ambitions for air power were political, to "bomb the head and not the tail". At the NATO summit on 21 April, he was granted his wish and the targets were widened to "turn out the lights in Belgrade", as the White House put it. Bombers could now hit power stations, bridges, trains, the media, factories and public buildings. At one point, the British tried to stop an attack on power lines that ran into Belgrade general hospital, but "were brought round".

By the start of May, NATO's promise of purely military targeting was a fiction. The ideology of strategic or "political" bombing was ascendant. Intensive bombing was intended to undermine civilian morale and force a change of policy, even of regime. Aerial assassination of Milošević and his family was attempted. An article in the current *Foreign Affairs* points out that bombing "objects indispensable to the survival of the civilian population" is a clear breach of the 1949 Geneva Convention. Yet from March onwards, NATO seemed unconcerned by legality. The UN's Mary Robinson was forced to remind the British Cabinet that it risked committing the same war crimes as Milošević.

As so often in history, the "logic of war" was more potent than its morality. Victory, it was hoped, would ask no questions. Britain's Defence Secretary, George Robertson, a bombing enthusiast, argued recently that bombing must have worked since Milošević capitulated. *Post hoc, ergo propter hoc*. NATO commanders on the ground will have none of this. What influenced Milošević, as [NATO's British commander on the ground] Lieutenant-General Sir Michael Jackson has often said, was proof that NATO finally had its act together for a land invasion. American concurrence was indicated to Milošević on 2 June, the day before he capitulated. At the same time, Milošević was told by Viktor Chernomyrdin that Moscow would not support him against such an invasion. Milošević now faced a real war, which he would lose. [General Wesley Clark, *Waging Modern War*; Andrew Gilligan, "Russia, not bombs, brought end to war in Kosovo, says Jackson", *Telegraph*, 1 August 1999].

There is no such thing as "immaculate coercion". Political bombing is a gesture of state violence, a harking back from modern war to the medieval terror of rape and pillage. The moral of Kosovo is that regulating other people's business should be done, if at all, with guns, tanks and soldiers, on the ground, properly, courageously and fast.

2

Marking Time: Interlude in Sierra Leone

At the start of 2000 Tony Blair soon had a new opportunity to pursue his mission in a more imperial theatre. A small group of British nationals, many involved in diamond mining, were caught up in a civil war in the former British colony of Sierra Leone, ill-protected by a small UN peace-keeping force. Their extraction to safety was declared a humanitarian necessity – though some subsequently denied they had requested it. Constant assurances were given that this was to be strictly a rescue mission, brief and with no danger of mission creep.

10.05.2000

ON 8 May the foreign secretary, Robin Cook, said that Britain would "not abandon its commitments to Sierra Leone". A spearhead battalion of 250 paratroops had already secured the airport outside the capital of Freetown to evacuate 500 British citizens. The paratroops will also offer support to the apparently helpless 8,000-strong United Nations force on the ground. Seven British warships, one armed with Harrier jets, are on the way to the area. Mr Cook's language and past actions suggest that they will stay a long time. He is the maestro of mission creep.

Hearing this week's news from West Africa, some might think that Britain's sole interest is to extract its nationals from a war-torn land. A unit of troops flies in, secures the airport, sets up a reception centre and evacuates the relevant passport-holders to a neighbouring safe haven. Those who dabble in African diamonds have always accepted risk. Not to mince words, they should be grateful that the British taxpayer is prepared to bail them out when the going gets hot.

Yet that is only front-of-stage. Britain is not going to Sierra Leone merely to evacuate its nationals. It is going there to show it cares about Africa, that wherever democracy is under threat and human lives are being lost, "something must be done". Why else has the carrier, HMS *Illustrious*, been diverted from duty? Why are 550 Marines setting sail this week from Marseilles aboard the helicopter carrier, HMS *Ocean*, as part of a full "Amphibious Ready Group", complete with the frigate, HMS *Chatham*, two Royal Fleet Auxiliary landing ships and a replenishment ship. Already four Chinooks are in theatre, alongside eight C130 Hercules.

Are they not enough? There are only 500 Britons in Sierra Leone. Many of those interviewed seem prepared to sit out the latest round of local mayhem, which has been continuous for almost a decade. What is going on?

The doctrine of overwhelming commitment is well-established in military circles, demonstrated in the Gulf War by General Colin Powell. It states that you always send more force than you are likely to need. Since politicians are as scared of casualties as are generals, and since the public never minds spending money on a shooting war, more force is duly sent. But is there no limit? "Overwhelming commitment" is always a temptation to over-commitment. Media attention goads escalation. Entry becomes ever easier, extrication ever harder.

I do not think Mr Cook or his colleagues are dishonest in telling the British people one thing – in Iraq or Kosovo or Sierra Leone – then doing something else. Politicians always take the line of least resistance. It starts with rhetoric, a flourish of "unacceptables", "intolerables" and "humanitarian outrages". Troops are alerted, pledged and then sent. They are accompanied by a heavy press contingent, eager for action. Mr Cook finds himself at summit conferences, in the spotlight, on television. Ultimatums are made. Critics of intervention are dismissed as cynics. Bombs are loaded. It all gets rather exciting.

Suddenly Britain is involved in a war in which its interests are minimal and nobody has the foggiest idea how to stop. Such intervention may do some good while it lasts, as did the American presence in Somalia. It rarely does good after it has gone. And go it one day must. Even this British Government does not plan to rule the world.

Fourteen years later, the British army is still in Sierra Leone, propping up the government of one of Africa's poorest states. The expedition did more than creep. It plunged in headlong. It stayed indefinitely. It was curious in that other opportunities to intervene and "nation build" elsewhere in sub-Saharan Africa were firmly resisted. Slaughter and genocide in Rwanda, Somalia, Sudan and Congo went deplored but ignored. It is hard to avoid the conclusion that Sierra Leone saw British intervention not to rescue white people but because it had once belonged to Britain. A similar motivation governed France's later intervention in a civil war in Mali, a former French colony. The age of intervention had acquired new protectorate.

Meanwhile across the Atlantic, Blair's plan for a new world order was being challenged from an unlikely quarter, the election of a Republican president. George W. Bush came to office on a firmly non-interventionist ticket. Blair's ideology of collective action by an international community was under threat. He even told his team, "We've got to turn these people into internationalists." The West's foreign policy seemed about to go into an isolationist phase. I was intrigued, indeed enthused, by Mr Bush's various foreign policy pronouncements. It seemed that the new age might come to an abrupt end.

15.12.2000

PRAISE BE, the age of cynical Western interventionism may be past. Yesterday saw the election of a new United States President, George W. Bush. The event could mean little or it could mean much. That is always the case when an empire changes hands. Millions may plod the same weary furrow, or they may suddenly die. Let us be optimistic.

Yesterday the old era displayed itself in symbolic finery. Bill Clinton visited Shakespeare's county of Warwickshire on his final lap of honour. These are the fanfares of a demi-paradise. "Let's purge this choler without letting blood", cries Mr Clinton to the cameras. In Belfast he tells the IRA to lay down its arms, the British to "demilitarise" and the Unionists to be patient. It is that easy. Everyone hugged and wept and was photographed. Times were so out of joint that Hillary Clinton actually kissed Martin McGuinness.

As Michael Ignatieff has argued in his book, *Virtual War,* the advent of smart weapons and "clean wars" has not lessened the inclination of the West to intervene. It has rather increased it. A President can order a bomber from Wisconsin to kill and flatten a target with impunity, in time for the evening news. Diplomacy, power projection and media manipulation all swill in the same opportunistic stew, without theme or legality. It is war as spectator sport, the politics of the Colosseum. Where next will a President wish to "walk tall"? Modern America can do what it likes, when it likes, where it likes, "born not to sue but to command".

George W. Bush has indicated, albeit in vague terms, an opposite tendency. He wants to see American troops return from Kosovo and Bosnia. He is sceptical of the buckets of aid tipped by the West into corrupt former communist regimes. He wants a European defence system firmly coupled to NATO. He wants American defence geared to America's interests, not to some "feel-good" humanitarianism.

The woman tipped as his National Security Adviser, Condoleezza Rice, and the probable new Secretary of State, Colin Powell, offer a distinct foreign policy from Mr Clinton's. According to a recent article by Ms Rice in the *Stanford Journal of International Relations,* the new Administration's priorities are military stability, world free trade and the spread of democratic values, in that order. Clinton/Blair humanitarian aggression is not on that list.

This explains why in future American troops should not find themselves "policing" the Balkans or Africa. It suggests that sanctions might be lifted from Iraq. Distant civil wars might be left to resolve themselves unaided, as did Lebanon's after the West withdrew in the 1980s. Human tragedies might again be for charities to combat. Humanitarianism might be privatised. At its most liberal, the policy might even leave South America free to grow products in such demand in America, without being devastated by the US Drug Enforcement Administration.

Some of this may be wishful thinking. Every President must head a coalition, Mr Bush more than most. The global intervention lobby will still be strong, a bizarre alliance of United Nations, aid agencies, arms manufacturers, soldiers and media propagandists. Against such imperialism, the voice of realpolitik and pragmatism will be small. The cry will always be "something must be done".

Yet every ideology has its antithesis. Mr Bush does not appear to be a man of bombast and show. He has (as yet) shown no sign of yearning the glamour and adulation of the foreign stage. Warwickshire is unlikely to be his first destination. His aides have shown themselves cautious men and women, capable of understanding the limits of "appropriate" intervention, of humility in the exercise of power. We can only hope.

That winter I found myself in south-east Asia, visiting the Laotian "backyard" of the Vietnam War along the Ho Chi Minh trail. It was a sobering place to contemplate the impact of so-called strategic bombing. A quarter century after the war it was still a traumatised landscape, devastated by surviving cluster munitions that continued to kill and maim local people. For all that, my reading of the Laotian campaign left traces of some of the strengths as well as the weakness in aerial warfare.

17.01.2001

WITH THE tenth anniversary of the Gulf War, and the second anniversary of the Yugoslav war looming, I last week visited the greatest bomb-site in history. It is the forgotten Plain of Jars, surely the world's most unobtrusive battlefield. For nine years, from 1964 to 1973, the tiny nation of Laos was bombed more ferociously than anywhere before or since. The bombing failed. Laos was not "bombed back to the Stone Age", as promised by US generals. It was merely bombed into communism. Communist it remains to this day.

The beautiful plain, in reality a long valley flanked by the high karst mountains, is still a morass of craters, each containing unknown, possibly unexploded, horrors. Its settlements were more blasted than the Somme, more flattened than Dresden. The 500-year-old provincial capital of Xiang Khouang saw its temples reduced to dust clouds by B52s. It was described afterwards as "looking like Hiroshima". Nobody knows how many people died. The only memorial I saw was to the 320 villagers of Tham Piu, forced from their homes into a cave, where a direct hit from a T28 rocket incinerated them. When the regimes of south-east Asia are told to hand over their "war criminals", they ask in sincere naivety: "Will Americans be there too?"

The Laos war was kept secret for six years, as the CIA and its special air force units had [in the late 1960s and early 1970s] supported local troops against the communist Pathet Lao and Vietcong. Though devoid of legal or moral justification, this initial period was an efficient war. Commanders freed of bureaucracy and political scrutiny fought well. Low-level strike aircraft were effective in close support of the Hmong ground troops. Laos was probably the last war in which airmen took greater risk than ground troops, notably the forward fire control Cessna pilots. Christopher Robbins's account of their war, *The Ravens*, is one of the best battlefield books I know.

Robbins's book is also a textbook on what air superiority can achieve, and what it cannot. Its villain is the US Air Force, whose incompetence in south-east Asia was of Crimean dimensions. By the time Nixon and Kissinger sent the Air Force's "strategic" B52s to the Plain of Jars in 1970 – against the pleading of their local commanders – the Vietnam War was lost. Punitive bombing exacted a terrible revenge on Laos, as on Cambodia to the south. Laos suffered a monsoon of destruction, with a peak of 500 sorties a day. The B52s used napalm, defoliants and weapons which, on any definition, were "chemical". They bombed the plain's Neolithic jars, like bombing Stonehenge. At night they hosed anything that moved with cannon. Yet the enemy calmly went on building roads and moving troops and supplies. The bombs were ineffective.

Laos showed the worth of close air support in the heat of battle. But this required pilots brave enough to engage the enemy with precision at close quarters. The politics of virtual war make this no longer an option. Pilots must fly high and safe. Smart missiles may nowadays compensate for the "lack of eyeball", but they require static targets, and besides the British RAF is too poor to afford many Tomahawks.

The contribution of bombing to the conflicts in Iraq and Yugoslavia has been heralded as a new era of risk-free, airborne coercion. Yet strategic bombing did not oust the Iraqis from Kuwait or the Serbs from Kosovo. This needed an actual or threatened ground assault. So-called strategic bombing of non-military targets in Serbia and Iraq did nothing to topple their respective regimes. Slobodan Milošević went only when voted from power and deserted by his army. Saddam Hussein is still there.

Laos, thank God, is recovering. But each week the echoes of that power [cluster bombs] still explode across its landscape, as they do across the plains of Iraq and Yugoslavia. Like medieval armies salting fields and poisoning wells, modern air forces leave behind them weapons which they know will sprout death for decades to come. I am told that not a single Cabinet minister protested against their use.

With the coming of a neo-isolationist American president, liberal debate on both sides of the Atlantic sought to redefine the new interventionism, as demonstrated in the successful air guaranteeing of Iraq and the occupying of Kosovo and Sierra Leone. In the eyes of Blair and his supporters this intervention, whether by the UN or NATO, would require championing in a Washington now averse to "world policing". I sought to set this new outlook in an historical context.

31.01.2001

THE *INTERNATIONAL Herald Tribune*, house journal of the new imperialism, carries articles almost daily by think-tankers and lobbyists explaining "what we must do" in some benighted corner of the globe. The cast of hobgoblins is devastating, from Saddam Hussein to North Korea, Latin American drug barons and African mass murderers. The movement is similar to the final decades of the British Empire, now being celebrated on the centenary of Queen Victoria's death. After decades of military and commercial supremacy came a last great burst of morality.

To Joseph Chamberlain, Lord Milner and the Round Table, "imperium" brought with it ethical obligations. The historian and novelist John Buchan wrote of nations that had lost their nerve and thus their sovereignty, much as we now talk of "failed states". Imperial rule was "the endless adventure", as young people now regard a stint with a UN agency or an NGO. To Milner, foreign affairs was the one dignified pursuit of the political elite.

Today is no different. From Cyprus and Gaza to Bosnia, Kosovo, East Timor and Sierra Leone the world is dotted with blue flags. Since the new imperialism never colonises, it need never decolonise. Its outposts are office blocks in every Third World capital. Its viziers live in hotel registers, club-class lounges and conference centres. This is an empire of virtue on which the sun never sets and in which any First World graduate can find a tax-free job. If Lenin were alive today he would find his "Imperialism as the Highest State of Capitalism" more pertinent than ever.

The British Empire gave way to the concept of national self-determination that underpinned the new United Nations. Decolonisation and the integrity of sovereign states was the ethos of the age. It was the ethos in which I was educated. Never did an ethos pass so quickly. You will encounter few articles or speeches in Britain or America these days espousing national self-determination. You will hear only the language of "something must be done" about foreign lands. This may involve the overthrow of a government (Iraq), or intervention in a civil war (Colombia), or the capture of a leader already declared guilty (Serbia), or merely the dislike of an election result (Austria). But something must always be done.

Despite a rising interest in intervention in Britain, I found no sign of it on a visit to Bush's home state of Texas in the spring of 2001. The experience of Somalia still rankled, reinforced by the release of the Ridley Scott film, _Black Hawk Down_. There was renewed tension in the Middle East at the time, with further argument over Iraq's supposed arsenal of weapons. Milošević had finally been toppled in Serbia. In China an American spy plane had crashed into an interceptor jet. For all these provocations, most Americans seemed content for their president to decline any invitation to take up "the white man's burden". I asked everyone what America should be doing about the ills of the world.

18.04.2001

THE ANSWER was simple. Nothing. What should he do about the rising tension in the Balkans? Nothing. Or about China, now that the spy plane crew were home? Nothing. Or about Iraq? Nothing. Or about Montenegro? Montenegro? Have another steak.

Every time a new President takes office, isolationism emerges from the stable and canters round the track. A new Republican President means "a period of retrenchment", because Republicans are cautious of overseas adventures. A new Democrat President means a period of introversion because "it's the economy, stupid". This seldom lasts. Events soon get the upper hand. But for a while the world has a nasty shock. Nanny is about to take time off, and the world must grow up on its own. It is a particularly nervy time for Britain, which likes always to peer from behind America's skirts and shout: "Go on, nanny, show 'em what for."

The last thing I saw on British television before crossing the Atlantic was a Rory Bremner sketch in which a dumb blonde wandered round the White House asking President Bush questions written to depict him as a right-wing dimwit. This is the America that makes Britons feel comfortable; America rich, strong and stupid. It is London as Athens to Washington's Rome. Americans can be as crazy as they like, so long as they smilingly help us out of our scrapes.

This stereotype could be in need of overhaul. The significant thing about the Chinese spy plane affair was not the efficiency and compromise with which it was resolved, but Mr Bush's behaviour. He did not grandstand. He did not go to Washington State to embrace the returning plane crew, as Bill Clinton would have done. He said that homecoming was for the crew and their families. Besides, the crisis had been managed by a team, with him as chairman. Nor had there been any leaks. Foreign policy was not about presidential machismo.

As for the Balkans, even the latest visit by the Secretary of State, Colin Powell, did little to dispel a general feeling that enough intervention is enough. As *The New York Times* Balkan correspondent, Steven Erlanger, wrote yesterday, the fall of Milošević has "clarified matters by stripping away any notion that outside intervention or the removal of one man alone can end the splintering and feuding in the Balkans". Erlanger adds that the West's 1999 intervention, "like the other great-power interventions of the last century, may have done more to destabilise the region than to stabilise it".

There are some voices from the past. The veteran diplomat Richard Holbrooke pleads for Mr Bush to adopt "a continued indeed increased American leadership role in the Balkans" [*New York Times*]. But to what end is not clear. The Balkans today are a threat to no one's peace but their own, a threat only exacerbated by the West's guns and money.

I can think of no contribution to this new thinking likely to come from Britain. Previously, every twist and publicity-seeking turn in Bill Clinton's foreign policy was slavishly applauded by Tony Blair and Robin Cook. Where he bombed, Britain bombed. Where he sanctioned, Britain sanctioned. Where he quit, Britain quit. London seems incapable of independent thought, let alone action, in foreign affairs. The one comfort is that, with Washington set on a new course, it will not take long for London to see its virtue.

That summer I wondered how long Bush's determination to hold aloof from the new intervention might last. The veterans of the Balkans and the foreign policy establishment still ached for American commitment to global policing. How long could Bush resist them? Eisenhower once said that the military-industrial complex was so strong that it would one day become the enemy of peace. The same was becoming true of a new "complex", that marshalling behind liberal imperialism, the UN, big aid and the media.

In any event, all these questions were brushed aside in one devastating morning in New York on September 11, 2001.

3

Eruption: Nine Eleven

Whether or not Osama bin Laden's attacks on the American mainland needed to transform the age of intervention, that is what they did. George W. Bush, initially traumatised, was soon a raging interventionist. For his part Tony Blair found for himself the role he craved as a global statesman. Within hours of the attack his biographer, Antony Seldon, reported that "he had his mind already on the world stage". Intervention took on a new potency and a new theme. For the time being it had nothing to do with humanitarianism.

I heard news of the twin-towers attack on returning from lunch in London. A phone call from the office told me to turn on my television and forget whatever I was writing for the following day's paper. I did so in time to watch the second plane smash into the World Trade Center. I was aghast. It was war, or at least terrorism, in real time. The information at my disposal was confused and partial. This is what I wrote between three o'clock and six o'clock that afternoon.

12.09.2001

FIRST THE horror. The attacks on the World Trade Center and Washington yesterday, before a horrified world, were the most vivid display of terror that I can recall. The heart of darkness had come to the heart of light and wreaked havoc.

New York is a city I love. It is bond-brother of London and cultural capital of a nation that has entered the new millennium as master of the world. That made it a natural target of envy and hatred. Those who question America's frequent global interventions in the cause of democracy do so always from a position of respect.

Leadership demands a price. When that price is paid in such symbolic centres of the nation as New York and Washington, Americans deserve every sympathy. Words may try to explain such events. None can justify them.

After the horror comes the response. The wise general always keeps in mind his enemy's objective. As with other recent attacks on Americans at home and abroad, the objective here cannot be the traditional one of those who wage violent war. It is not to defeat America, to undermine its economic power or military strength, nor even to damage its political stability. Such goals are unachievable. That is why comparisons with Pearl Harbor are silly. The objective is to humiliate America and goad her into a violent response.

To achieve this goal requires more than a big bang. It requires that bang to be publicised and for the reaction to it to be equally violent. Its effectiveness lies not in the death toll – a toll repeated daily on the roads – but in the loudness of the echo through the world's media. It lies in the action replay, the humanising of the tragedy, the publicity for those responsible. It lies in the aftermath.

There is no military defence against attacks such as these. Indeed there is no realistic defence at all. America will doubtless redouble its efforts to penetrate and contain the groups responsible. But they will not be defeated by main force. Any plane can be hijacked. Any building is vulnerable. People can be protected individually but not in the mass. A community can always be gassed or poisoned.

The paradox of new technology is that it makes developed states more vulnerable to random assault. In the war of the weak against the strong, the weak can wield weapons more potent than ever before. Globalisation may render the rich richer and the poor poorer. But it offers the self-appointed champions of the poor devastating means of forcing their attention on the world.

Faced with horrors such as these, "anti-missile" defence systems seem suddenly obsolete. No rogue state needs an intercontinental ballistic missile to assault America when a boy with a suitcase or a suicide hijacker can walk through any shield. A trillion dollars hurled into outer space cannot stop the blast of a civilian jet loaded with fuel out of Boston airport. Fylingdales may detect a menace from outer space, but not a virus in a handbag or a madman in Club Class.

To protect every American building is clearly impossible. To attempt to protect city centres against suicide attack plays the attacker's game. It awards him the attention he craves, the apotheosis of fame. The constant search for security becomes a ghostly re-enactment of the outrage, a reminder and a challenge to next time. That surely is why the World Trade Center was targeted for a second time. It added an eerie echo to the "ripple" of the terror. Its power lies in the memory of blood-stained bodies and sobbing women, of shattered buildings and a world turned upside down.

If yesterday's acts were committed under the sponsorship of a foreign state, retaliation might be understandable. But punitive action requires a collective entity that can be held responsible. Here there are only shadowy groups, moving from country to country, terrifying their hosts as much as the rest of the world. In 1993 the World Trade Center was the victim of a massive car bomb. It appeared to be the work of Arab fundamentalists with ties to Afghanistan and Sudan. No conceivable response to the attack made any sense, except to track down the individuals concerned. They appear to have struck again.

The non-interventionist might argue that incidents such as these can be avoided. They would plead with America not to intervene everywhere and thus render its territory a target to all whom its government has offended abroad. This argument must be met since many enemies of America will cite it. They will point out that the scenes on television yesterday were different only in degree from those experienced by civilian victims of American bombing in Yugoslavia and Iraq. Those critical of NATO bombing might offer America more sympathy if NATO had offered sympathy for the hundreds of civilian deaths from its missiles and cluster bombs far from home. US generals openly demanded the bombing of civilian targets in Belgrade and Baghdad, to "break the will" of local people. Is that not what the perpetrators of yesterday's outrage might say?

Here we tread warily. Sponsoring the state of Israel led America into a prolonged and senseless hostility to the cause of the dispossessed Palestinians. The financing of anti-Soviet warlords in Afghanistan in the 1980s armed and galvanised terrorist groups, including Osama bin Laden and others behind the 1993 bombing of the World Trade Center. The criminalisation by the Americans of the trade in heroin and cocaine, of which America is the major consumer, ensures that crime triumphs in states throughout Asia and South America. The continuance of the Kuwaiti policing operation into weekly bombing of Iraq has made Saddam a regional hero and America an object of regional hatred.

To seek revenge would be senseless. America showed after attacks on its East African embassies in 1998 that it regards revenge as a legitimate weapon in its geopolitical arsenal. The [previous] bombing of Afghanistan was ineffective. That of Sudan was illegal and militarily indefensible. Revenge is not the response of a sophisticated political community. America above all should know Thomas Paine's plea, to "lay the axe to the root and teach governments humanity . . . sanguinary punishments corrupt mankind".

To react to an atrocity by abandoning the customary self-control of democracy is to help the terrorist to do his work. He wants America to behave as the regional bully of local demonology. To extend further America's Middle East economic sanctions, isolation and military aggression offers succour to the terrorist. These policies have not hastened the spread of democracy or stability through the region. They have, if anything, done the reverse. They should be replaced with policies of engagement, trade, friendship and contact.

The message of yesterday's incident is that, for all its horror, it does not and must not be allowed to matter. It is a human disaster, an outrage, an atrocity, an unleashing of the madness of which the world will never be rid. But it is not politically significant. It does not tilt the balance of world power one inch. It is not an act of war. America's leadership of the West is not diminished by it. The cause of democracy is not damaged, unless we choose to let it be damaged. Maturity lies in learning to live, and sometimes die, with the madmen.

The events of 9/11 saw an outpouring of sympathy for America that is hard today to recall. Messages of support came from almost every country on earth, including Russia and China, excluding only such sworn foes as Iraq and Afghanistan. The PLO leader, Yasser Arafat, gave blood for the people of New York. All the world claimed "to be American". Even the Taliban leadership was so shocked as to summon a *loya jirga* (tribal conclave) to discuss what

to do about their al-Qaeda guests in the Tora Bora mountains. Many younger leaders were reported to have pressed for them to leave. They were now "unwelcome guests".

How would America use this outpouring of sympathy? The answer would surely dictate how long it lasted. In London Blair was suddenly galvanised into diplomatic activism. Initially he pleaded caution to his American friends.

14.09.2000

THE WORLD is seeing America at its best. Those whom Britain honoured in London yesterday and will honour in Parliament today are Americans that Britons know and admire. They have a capacity for communal grief that does not neglect individual tragedy. They know the meaning of restraint. Their humanity is not outstripped by hysteria. Britain too has been a nation pounded by terror and can offer the sympathy of experience. The special relationship is bonded, if bond is needed, by the many Britons who also died on Tuesday.

The world is apprehensive. It prays that it is not about to see a different America. That country is rattling every sabre and girding itself for war. Wretched people in wretched cities across the Middle East are burying themselves in bunkers. A global armada is on full alert. Nobody doubts America's power to visit unimaginable violence on others. But to what end? Americans are angry but surely not stupid. They can distinguish determination from vengeance, caution from appeasement, acts of will from acts of idiocy.

What an argument looms ahead, what a ghastly parting of the ways beckons. The debate over how to react to the Manhattan slaughter could yet hew NATO in half and unleash mayhem across half the world. The resulting carnage could even drive America, still global guarantor of democracy, back behind its borders for a generation. Such a catastrophe would be caused not by the perpetrators of this week's outrage. They deserve no such place in history. The cause would be faulty analysis and reactive warmongering by the world's most powerful nation.

In the aftermath of horror, heart rules head. But head must reassert itself. Listening and reading this past two days has left me appalled at the hawkishness of pundits, politicians and commentators. They are the true destabilisers, the menaces to peace. Of course they must struggle to reflect the disgust felt by powerless citizens. They must hear the cry for authority to reassert control and for justice to be swift. But the statesman's job is not to rant but to think, to channel understandable emotion into reasoned action. It is weakness that jerks the knee and drops the bomb.

American and British leaders (though not Tony Blair) have sonorously declared that "democracy is at war". This cannot be sensible. War is a "forcible contention between states". Neither America nor Britain, let alone worldwide democracy, is more at risk this week than last. Thousands have died, along with their murderers. Buildings are vulnerable, but not states and ideologies. What good is served by pretending otherwise? The same target – the World Trade Center – was attacked in 1993 but failed to collapse. That act could have been equally lethal, but war was not declared. The success of an atrocity does not turn a terrorist into a warrior or his mob into a state.

There is no coherent use for the mass of weaponry being mobilised by America and her allies in the Pacific, Atlantic and Indian oceans. The US Secretary of State, Colin Powell, has promised "more than a single reprisal raid". Hundreds of dead Afghans will not right the wrongs of Manhattan, though it might spark a further round of tit-for-tat atrocities. Hawks such as Al Haig and Britain's Lord Powell of Bayswater demand an "overwhelming response" as a means of "deterring these madmen". Suicidal madmen are not deterred.

Even the terrorist is a politician. He swims in a sea of hatred and clings to rafts of grievance. The Americans have reportedly been shocked at how widely disliked they are in the Middle East. They seem unaware of the impact on their image of decades of anti-Palestinian partisanship and of the bombing and impoverishment of Iraq. Until this dislike is tackled, the co-operation essential to rooting out terrorism is unrealistic.

A great assault on Muslim states from the air would be the answer to bin Laden's prayer. Fanatics would flock to his cause. To many Arabs it would seem to legitimise the Manhattan slaughter. NATO revenge raids would not only lower the West to the same barbarism as was shown by the terrorist. It could hardly be more counter-productive to the anti-terrorist cause.

These dreadful people seek neither wealth nor territory, only fame for their cause. They need sanctuary. But the Russians spent a decade trying to flush them from the Afghan mountains and were condemned by the West for their troubles. That conflict destroyed a moderate regime and created a fanatical one, from groups recklessly financed by the Americans. The British Empire met its Waterloo on the North-West Frontier. So did the Russian Empire. Are the Americans about to follow?

The attack on 9/11 was to be the fulcrum on which the age of intervention turned. There was no longer any concern for humanitarianism. Afghanistan, host to al-Qaeda's leadership, was in America's cross hairs. There was no assessment of the West's interests in Afghanistan or its neighbouring states. Within a week America's mood changed and revenge became a political craving. It was one that Washington found hard to resist. Yet revenge against whom?

19.09.2001

AT THE weekend, American pollsters asked their public how their Government should react to Tuesday's attacks in New York and Washington. Eighty-five per cent of respondents supported military action. An astonishing 58 per cent wanted action "even if it means that many thousands of innocent civilians may be killed". These were not Viking berserks. They were sophisticated Americans. Most would have called themselves Christians.

As of today, the American Government has, to its credit, not responded to this call. Its language of total war may have gladdened the heart of Osama bin Laden and his supporters, as must the stock market panic, the travel embargoes and the nonsense cries that "nothing will ever be the same again". But the leash of common sense still restrains the dog of war. Bin Laden had laid his trap. He has filled it with bloody and provocative bait. He is watching and waiting.

The West's leaders have so far refused to respond. Their rhetoric is terrorising the Afghan people into fleeing their homes. But they have not done the stupidest thing on Earth and granted bin Laden his holy war. They have resisted the pseudo-macho, tactically incoherent euphemisms for such a war, the demands to "hang tough", "show balls" and "teach lessons", demands that pass for strategy among brains softened by decades of peace.

The cynical purpose of declaring war on terrorism, like the abortive "war on drugs", is to silence such critics and harness emotion to the cause of policy. It puts reason in quarantine. We should therefore be aware how thin is the veneer of democratic culture. A few crazed individuals can apparently induce great nations to suppress their instinct for justice, replacing it with quotes from *Henry V*.

Three weeks after the 9/11 attack, the temperature was rising on both sides of the Atlantic. Blair was flying frantically between Arab capitals, seeking a coalition that might induce the Afghan Taliban to hand over bin Laden. Intelligence indicated this might happen but would take time. American opinion was disinclined to wait.

26.09.2001

LAWRENCE OF Arabia's *Seven Pillars of Wisdom* is an epic tale of Western engagement in Arabia, one of the most dramatic and romantic tales of men in conflict. Its message for the present is clear: always fight Arabs with Arabs and always keep your word. Reading the book this weekend, I wondered if anyone in charge was doing the same. Have British ministers or commanders heard of Lawrence? Do they think he was merely a star in a camel movie?

The Bush administration has respected Lawrence's warning up to a point. It did not do what Bill Clinton would have done. Hawks in the Pentagon (and in the British press) wanted Clinton-style punitive bombing raids on Kabul. George Bush refused. There could be no faster way of exhausting sympathy and support in the region, no surer way of endangering any mission to extract Osama bin Laden from his hide. Mr Bush's team of Gulf War veterans – the same as wisely counselled against seizing Baghdad in 1991 – remains a talisman of sanity in this bizarre affair.

The declared objective is still to find, arrest and bring to trial the man thought to be responsible for the New York and Washington atrocities. The objective is just. The crime was never "an assault on democracy". If Western democracy cannot withstand a suicide bomb attack on an office block, it is pathetic indeed. The crime was directed not against democracy but against Western policies in the Middle East. To mis-describe it is to inflate and thus appease the terrorist. But the culprit must be found. The question is how, and are there means proportionate to ends?

Getting Arabs to arrest bin Laden, somehow, some day, was always the best response to the American atrocities. If that could not be achieved, then a daring in-and-out raid would have to do. But to cover such a raid by in effect declaring war on an Arab state and toppling its government can only suck the West into a trap. It risks the wealth of sympathy that America has garnered this past fortnight and could yet destroy the world coalition [of sympathisers with America] to which Tony Blair yesterday drew attention and for which he can take considerable credit.

This credit was to be soon exhausted. By the first week in October all Blair's apparent advocacy of restraint had come to nothing. The targets were selected and the bombers in place. Despite continuing his whirlwind visits, Blair was turning from dove to hawk. In his Labour Party conference speech that month he went into interventionist overdrive, talking of a coming war as, "a moment to seize. The kaleidoscope has been shaken. The pieces are in flux. Soon they will settle again. Before they do so, let us reorder the world around us."

This was bizarre grandiloquence. The age of intervention was about to explode onto a higher plane than the fumbling humanitarianism of Yugoslavia and the macho bombing of Iraq. Britain was to join America in a war on a Muslim state and there was no other motive than pure revenge.

10.10.2001

THE FACES of Britain's rulers on Monday night said it all. They had lost an argument. Sitting in Parliament they looked haggard and wretched. Tony Blair thumped on yet again about Osama bin Laden being a fiend and a monster. Everyone chanted that bombing should be "proportionate, measured, targeted", knowing that this was beyond their control. Clare Short's face was a picture of misery. She must now excuse the civilian deaths, the laying of cluster mines, the airborne terror for which she is responsible as a War Cabinet member. How skin-deep is humanity when the guns begin to fire. Whenever Americans start bombing, Britons dive under a blanket of Churchillian waffle.

Britain is not at war at present, any more than it was at war during the IRA bombing of London or after bin Laden's previous attack on New York's World Trade Center. To describe what should be a relentless campaign against criminal terror as war is metaphor abuse. By hurling resources and media attention at some distant theatre, it deflects effort from the domestic front. It also insults those who fought and died in real wars, when territory was threatened and states were at risk.

For the past three weeks, the case against bombing was marshalled in every capital in the world. It was advanced in Washington itself by Colin Powell and Condoleezza Rice. Tony Blair's every waking hour was devoted to it. His round-the-clock diplomacy was to build up the case for "cunning not killing", not in the Middle East but in Washington. He was sincere but eventually he lost.

Blair was to continue his diplomacy round the capitals of the Middle East, aimed at securing the capture of bin Laden. It was futile. The Taliban was beyond reach. Blair now appeared little more than the poodle of an imminent American war. It was one that he had struggled to avert but in which he now seemed almost desperate to join alongside America. He was adamant that British planes join the first sorties against Kabul.

02.11.2001

IN 1853 the explorer Richard Burton became the first Westerner to penetrate the holy shrine of Mecca. He afterwards warned a follower: "Those who find danger the salt of pleasure may visit Mecca. But if asked whether the result justifies the risk, I should reply in the negative." Tony Blair this week cast himself as Burton. By all accounts, his last voyage to the Middle East was brave, miserable and fruitless. Critics castigated it as a humiliating blunder. I disagree, but only if the outcome justifies the risk and defies Burton's admonition.

No British leader has performed such intensive personal diplomacy in the region before, let alone on behalf of a foreign power. Arab commentators have reflected that Osama bin Laden must indeed be a man of substance to make a Briton pay court to the murky rulers of Damascus, Amman and Riyadh. No French, German or even Russian leader would attempt such desperate intervention. Yet it is hard not to admire a prime minister who, having cast himself as Richard the Lionheart, then tests the role to destruction.

Mr Blair's visa was stamped "Ambassador Unplenipotentiary to the USA". Yet that country left him woefully shorn of support. At his moment of maximum exposure in Syria, Washington ordered a B52, the veteran symbol of American militarism, to begin the "carpet-bombing" of Afghanistan. The snub could hardly have been more blatant. As the Pentagon's Paul Wolfowitz indicated on British television that night, allies, coalitions and diplomacy are of no concern to him. He welcomes Mr Blair's unflagging support, as do all Americans. But should Britons object to his strategy, they can get lost. They will be labelled wobbly, appeasers and "soft on terror". To the Pentagon, Mr Blair's job in the Middle East was a bomb salesman.

Assuming they proceed to topple the Afghan regime, America and Britain will have to sustain a miserable and bloody puppet government in Kabul under perpetual siege from its neighbours. They will have granted bin Laden or his successors what he craves, an anti-American coalition across the "crescent of instability". They will have created and then wrecked a bond of shared purpose between Christian and Muslim worlds, forged by a global horror at September 11.

4

Into Afghanistan

The American and British bombing of Kabul and other Afghan cities began on 7 October, less than four weeks after 9/11. It was with UN authorisation under the auspices of NATO. Operation Enduring Freedom caused widespread destruction of Afghan cities but failed to dent Taliban defences north of Kabul. It was hoped that units of the mostly Tajik Northern Alliance, long enemies of the Taliban, would now move south to seek revenge for al-Qaeda's murder of their leader, Ahmad Shah Massoud, shortly before 9/11. The Americans were eager not to commit ground forces and were anyway chiefly obsessed with finding Osama bin Laden.

The Northern Alliance was reluctant to move until given tactical air support by the Americans. This was duly supplied, with devastating attacks on Taliban positions with cluster bombs, daisy cutters and attack helicopters. It still took six weeks for Kabul to fall, on 12 November. But when it did, it fell suddenly and the Taliban retreated to its base in Kandahar. No one quite knew what should happen next.

14.11.2001

COMMANDERS HATE the unpredictable. Until two days ago, the strategy being touted in London and Washington was of a Western ground assault on Afghanistan postponed until the spring. High altitude "psychological" bombing would assuage the Americans' need for reprisal. This might undermine regional support, but American commanders would not commit troops to a grizzly and possibly inconclusive ground war over the winter. Patience must be the keyword. Something might turn up.

Something has turned up. The much-feared Taliban proved completely flaky. Whatever the political counter-productivity of bombing civilian targets in Kabul and Kandahar, close air support for Northern Alliance troops on the front line was clearly effective. The troops, re-equipped and goaded forward by American "advisers", were eager to avenge past humiliation at the hands of the Taliban, not least the murder of their Tajik leader, Ahmed Shah Massaud. Having chosen to ride this particular tiger, America and Britain must do so.

I hope the word ethical never again crosses the lips of a British minister. Not in modern history can Britain have forged an alliance with such unsavoury characters as Abdul Rashid Dostum, Abdul Malik, Ismail Khan, Mohammad Ustad Atta and other northerners, mostly financed by heroin. These men have given a new dimension to the word terror. Ahmed Rashid's admirable book, *Taliban*, should be avoided by any squeamish coalition partner. Yes, Kabul has been liberated, but as Mr Rashid makes plain, it is by the same gangs whose faction-fighting and brutality gave the Taliban their opportunity seven years ago.

These men make Slobodan Milošević look like a playground bully and Hamas and Hezbollah a couple of lightweights. Their greed for drugs money is outstripped only by their retributive sadism. Rape, mutilation and the most gruesome executions are, as Edward Gibbon would say, only the lesser charges that General Dostum might in rights have to answer before a war crimes tribunal. He never will. These men are "us" and "our allies in the coalition against terror". They quaff vodka with British and American special forces. Such is the moral relativism of war.

The past month has shown a West pathetically vulnerable to fear. It refuses to travel. It avoids tall buildings. It sees infinite menace in subway trains, bridges, food supplies, even the air it breathes. It plunges its economy into self-induced recession. Pathologically risk-averse, we demand of our rulers degrees of protection that only a totalitarian state can offer. Perhaps it is small wonder that Mr Bush and Mr Blair react by declaring a Hundred Years War on an abstract noun, terrorism.

I was brought up to believe that Western civilisation was too robust to be threatened by this sort of terrorism. I thought that British democracy was strong enough not to glorify bin Laden as a Hitler, summoning a "war cabinet" against him and flattering him with overblown "emergency powers". The West is weaker than I thought. But Afghanistan will test that weakness. It will test the new moral imperialism more severely than did Vietnam, the Balkans or recent excursions into the Middle East. Afghanistan's history says that this adventure will end in tears. In Kabul we must fight more than terrorism. We must fight history.

The fall of Kabul put the city, and notionally the country, under a UN "transitional administration". An interview with a former Afghan diplomat in London convinced me that the Taliban had been sufficiently split on hosting bin Laden that it needed only time to spring him. Indeed he told me bin Laden was already a dead man for the murder of the Tajik leader, Shah Massoud.

A post-9/11 *loya jirga* at Kandahar saw younger Taliban commanders (some in contact with Americans since the 1990s) furious at their leader Mullah Omar continuing to give hospitality to bin Laden and his alien Arabs. They secured a request, unenforced, that he leave. [Lucy Morgan Edwards, *The Afghan Solution*, Bacteria 2011.]

As it was, America and Britain "took ownership" of a distant foreign state. As in Bosnia and Kosovo, the age of intervention had led from military victory to military occupation to de facto political responsibility. Afghanistan was not, like Yugoslavia, a developed European state. Outside Kabul it was one of the world's poorest and least developed nations, its economy heavily reliant on heroin exports. In December an interim government under the Pashtun leader, Hamid Karzai, was installed, heavily dependent on outside administrators.

By the following May, differences of policy began to emerge between America and Britain. These seemed a matter of political culture. America was eager to extricate itself from what it saw as a punitive man hunt, as yet unsuccessful. Britain was instinctively imperialist.

It was eager to take territory and engage in national reconstruction. A sign of this fantasy was that a British minister, Clare Short, was assigned to ending the country's dependence on poppies.

22.05.2002

THE REPORT ran: "Akbar Khan, heir to the Afghan throne, was forced by his British conquerors to wander the wilderness in exile, plotting his revenge ... A swarthy horseman galloped towards him bringing news. The garrison of Kabul had been depleted. The Afghan tribes were in revolt. They had written their oaths in blood on the leaves of the Koran. Akbar's dark eyes glowed. His powerful sensual mouth uttered fierce orders." By the time he had driven the Infidel back through the Khyber, 20,000 Britons were dead.

We do not report wars like that anymore. But British troops still scramble over Afghan ravines, "denying" them to tribesmen for a month or two to keep London happy. I doubt if any expedition has ever been sent on a mission so militarily obscure and so politically blatant as the present Marine operation in Shah-i Kot. What are these troops doing? The Taliban has been toppled, so easily as to amaze all but those who know their Taliban. As long as the West is meddling, Afghan politics has returned to lawlessness, whether financed by drugs or aid. Al-Qaeda has shifted its headquarters to Pakistan and a dozen other places. The Marines can do no more than obey their covert orders. These are to find a proper firefight, take casualties as predicted by ministers, declare a victory and return home in glory.

Why? The Americans have all but given up the fight in Afghanistan. Their abortive bid to find Osama bin Laden ended in the same Shah-i Kot district now being scoured by British troops. They were badly shot up and left with eight dead. After the failure of Operation Anaconda, George Bush asked Tony Blair to take their place. He in turn asked the Marines, who declined to move for a month.

The Americans are now openly saying they have "no dog in the Afghan fight". Last October can be seen for what it always was, a punitive revenge raid for domestic consumption. Finding Osama bin Laden was not a priority, since Pakistani negotiations with the Taliban and Saudi Arabia on his extradition were then on a knife-edge. The story is told by Rohan Gunaratna of St Andrew's University in his remarkable new study, *Inside Al Qaeda* (Hurst). The bombing wrecked the negotiations and abruptly cemented a weakening alliance between the unpopular al-Qaeda and the Taliban in Kabul. That did not matter to the Americans. Bombing mattered.

Today the reconstruction of Afghanistan is no longer America's business. Nor are conditions in the appalling prisons of Britain's so-called ally, General Dostum. Nor is the reopening of the opium warehouses and the falling price of European heroin. Nor is the fate of Kabul's hapless Hamid Karzai, desperate for Western troops to hold territory outside his capital. Afghanistan may still be host to the world's "special forces", eager for bounty or glory. But the country is off the political map.

The truth is that America's war aim, unlike Britain's, was coherent. It was to hit hard and get out. Americans are not complaining about the Taliban "refusing to confront Our Boys and fight". They are not complaining that we cannot "tell friend from foe" or that "they keep returning to their villages", all reported comments of British Marines last week. Americans are not staying around to police the unpoliceable. Once it was clear that Osama bin Laden was not to be found, the US declared the battle won. Mr Blair can tell the Afghans that "Britain will not desert you" but President Bush has moved elsewhere.

I doubt if Mr Cheney was bluffing last week to divert attention from allegations of White House negligence prior to September 11. But his constant terrifying of hypersensitive Americans does al-Qaeda's job for it. An al-Qaeda memorandum after September 11 gloated that Americans were now so scared that the Intercontinental had to lay off 20,000 employees, "thanks to Allah's grace". Al-Qaeda can tax the American economy billions of dollars merely by getting Mr Cheney to do its work for it.

The challenge is therefore the same as it was before September 11. It is to find and eliminate terrorists in each and every Western state. This is difficult given the freedoms that the West holds sacred, but to sacrifice these freedoms is to let the terrorist win. Not to sacrifice them is to risk another outrage. Democracy is always a balancing of evils. But Afghanistan is nothing to do with the case.

Despite America's political reluctance, American and British troops continued to campaign to pacify the Afghan countryside through the summer of 2002. They were joined by some two dozen NATO and other countries under pressure to broaden the base of the "coalition". Since most of these were sent on the strict understanding that they would not fight, NATO's headquarters in Kabul took on something of the air of an international holiday - camp.

The justification for the intervention duly became ever more high-flown. The "War on Terror" was presented as comparable to great wars of the past. Bin Laden was regularly compared with Hitler. Going to Afghanistan was a crusade, a sacred duty for the defenders of democracy everywhere, with Kabul as its Jerusalem. Humanitarian motives became uppermost in this presentation. The campaign was about lifting a nation out of the middle ages, relieving the suffering of women and stabilising a region. NATO was acting not just as policeman but as harbinger of democracy and a welfare state.

12.06.2002

I CANNOT see anything remotely comparable to Hitler or Soviet communism in the threat from al-Qaeda. I disagree that the traditional state is decaying. The end of the Cold War has seen the revival, not the demise, of nationhood. Territorial self-determination remains the underpinning of democracy. It instigated the justified war to rescue Kuwait and was NATO's battle cry in the Balkans.

The great wars of the twentieth century were real wars. They threatened the existence of states with subjugation and slavery. The need to eradicate al-Qaeda is serious. But al-Qaeda's success was in large part the result of a failure of American policy, both in domestic intelligence and in appeasing Saudi Arabia in the 1990s. Such a threat must be fought, but as a criminal conspiracy not a war of states.

The world is vastly more peaceful and stable than at any time in modern history. It has no need of new bogeys to fuel the military industrial complex. No member of George Bush's "axis of evil" could plausibly overthrow the British or American Governments. If there is an al-Qaeda "British cabinet-in-waiting" it is a Chestertonian fantasy. Of course biological and chemical weapons constitute a menace. They are lethal to people, as is any criminal act or natural disaster. But they are not "lethal to society".

Americans see this differently because they have so little experience of political violence. I value America's role as a global intervener as a last resort. That is why I worry when it seems to lose the ability to grade a threat. This becomes dangerous when exaggeration begins to sound like crying wolf. Those in Washington now predicting imminent atrocity every week will soon find people no longer listening. When they stop listening they start dropping their guard.

5

Back to Iraq

As America began to lose interest in Afghanistan, there was no sign of George W. Bush reverting to his former isolationism. Just the reverse. There were signs of a revival of Washington's obsession with Iraq. Britain's interest was obscure. Indeed it was largely confined to Tony Blair himself, usually following his periodic visits to Bush in America. It did not include the British Foreign Office or defence ministry, both appalled by talk of an attack on Iraq. By July 2002 the prime minister's personal fixation was coming into the open and causing nervousness among his colleagues.

31.07.2002

THIS IS becoming surreal. Soldiers do not want a war. Diplomats do not want a war. Politicians do not want a war. This is exactly how wars start.

When Tony Blair was asked at a press conference last week about an early attack on Iraq his body language went absent without leave. His cheek muscles twitched, his eyes darted and he reached beneath his desk for help. Was he seeking a panic button or a White House messenger? The answer was worse. He raised a comfort mug to hide his lips and took a large caffeine hit. He stumbled out a no comment.

I cannot recall a time when British policy towards a troubled part of the world was so incoherent. Mr Blair has no clue what America intends to do in Iraq. This is understandable since, as yet, nor does America. But other governments are not thereby reduced to treating their publics as idiots. Britons are served a burble of "no decision ... not ready ... weapons of mass destruction ... regime change in Baghdad ... nothing imminent". Yet every leak suggests a Government preparing for war. Mr Blair is like an East European leader in the

Soviet era, forced to support anything Moscow does without knowing what it is.

Let us help poor Mr Blair in his predicament. Let us examine the case for a war. The customary reason would be that Saddam Hussein threatens the security of the British State and the lives of its citizens. Mr Blair has been unable to convince anyone of this. He must therefore fall back on a generalised threat posed by the Iraqi leader to the outside world, one so grave as to justify early military intervention.

The ghosts of Beau Geste and Lawrence of Arabia are stalking the war rooms of NATO. What to the country at large may seem unreal and implausible is, to Mr Blair, a desperate crisis. As he puts it over and again, despite a decade of containment "inaction is not an option".

The first objection to any war is that it may be lost. The American military has a dreadful record in trying to topple declared enemies. In Cuba, Libya, Somalia, Serbia and now Afghanistan, a named individual was targeted and survived. Assassination attempts against Castro, Gaddafi, Aideed, Milošević and bin Laden gave all of them a sudden elixir of life. Aideed died in his bed. Milošević lost power only to a democratic vote. The rest are going strong. As Gaddafi might reflect, an American precision bomb is the next best thing to immortality.

America can surely defeat Iraq. While President Bush may survive his failure to capture bin Laden, he could hardly excuse a failure to eliminate Saddam when "regime change" was his sole objective. Provided an invasion is sufficiently massive, there is no reason why "the mother of all victories" should not be achieved. The Republican Guard may exact a heavy price. But with Baghdad laid to waste and to hell with collateral damage, regime change is surely do-able.

A second objection to a war is whether, though winnable, it is "legal". To that we may reply, so what? No particular legality attached to the bombing of Belgrade or Kabul, in both of which Britain participated. As America has made plain, it regards international jurisprudence as a discipline for losers, not winners. George Bush and his defence secretary, Donald Rumsfeld, never cease to assert that war on Iraq is not an act of international policing, requiring United Nations authorisation. It is a matter of American self-defence. In such cases, international law is indulgent.

This may not help Mr Blair. He appears to see this war as part self-defence but part moral crusade. For the latter he needs more authority than a phone call from Mr Bush, especially as he means to disregard his own parliament. But a poodle knows only one master. I suspect that the United Nations will not feature prominently in Britain's "war aims" against Iraq.

A third objection to war is quite different – that all my assumptions above are not true and that a war is unnecessary. The threatened aggression which it means to forestall is not real. The evidence is not sufficient to justify bloodshed and destruction. This objection would point out that the containment policy towards Iraq has not failed. It has merely not succeeded. After the Gulf War, America made a mistake. It should have treated Saddam as it now treats Libya, Syria, Iran and other dictatorships, and as it once treated Saddam himself. It should have smothered him with "constructive engagement". That was the way to keep tabs on him. To attack Iraq when Saddam's standing is high in the region is to fan the flames of anti-Americanism and set al-Qaeda back on the recruiting path.

I would love to see Saddam go. He is a thoroughly nasty job of work with a nasty arsenal at his disposal. I would scheme in every way to bring about his downfall. But Britain must have a *casus belli*, a reason to wage aggression against a foreign state. Mr Blair has none.

We now know that over the autumn of 2002 Blair was in secret talks to prepare for war with Iraq with Bush and his team. He was acutely aware that he would lack cabinet or political support for this, especially as UN weapons inspectors were going in to and out of Iraq regularly and reporting nothing that could pass for "weapons of mass destruction". Blair duly went to unprecedented lengths to prepare opinion for possible military action. This included the promise of an unprecedented intelligence "dossier" revealing the scale of the threat posed by Saddam.

04.09.2002

WHERE OH where is a Third Way on Iraq? The discomfort of Britain's prime minister on the dominant issue of the day is moving over the pain threshold. As George W. Bush fortifies the OK-Corral for a fight, Tony Blair races to proclaim his 100 per cent support, declaring that "doing nothing is not an option". Yet he remains unable to say what that something might be. He seems a man in tormented suspense, awaiting a sign from across the pond.

America's position on a war against Iraq is clear. It is undecided. That is the privilege of the powerful. Whether from art or necessity, Mr Bush is keeping his options open. With his advisers deeply divided over going to war, he has sensibly taken refuge in "patience". Any fool can smash Iraq to bits. Any fool may even topple President Saddam Hussein. But whether that really makes the world a safer place remains moot.

Mr Blair now says that he will publish a "dossier" proving not just that Saddam has unpleasant weapons but that he has the means and, in some sense, the intention to use them. We can only sit and wait, wondering why so vital a basis for a *casus belli* has taken so long to prepare and why the Americans, under similar pressure of public opinion, have not themselves published it.

To validate a pre-emptive war against a foreign state requires at least some clear evidence of a proposed attack and a failure to honour an ultimatum. Nobody thought of attacking Pakistan when it acquired a nuclear bomb. Iraq must threaten someone to merit the catastrophic destruction of modern war. This is not a game of hunt the Churchill quote.

After September 11 a year ago, Mr Blair flew round the world in an impressive act of diplomacy. He forged a "coalition against terror" that had Russia, China and almost the entire Arab world on America's side. That coalition was initially crucial to the global campaign against al-Qaeda, a campaign that has yet to succeed.

Now the coalition could not speak more clearly. It regards as a dangerous distraction the war which Mr Bush is actively planning and Mr Blair is ready to support. To try to remove Saddam by force without calling his latest bluff on weapons inspection or seeking widespread support through the UN would undo all that Mr Blair and others achieved a year ago. It might possibly remove one threat to Western interests. It would certainly generate another.

The first anniversary of 9/11 saw much reflection worldwide on the event and its aftermath. Operation Anaconda in Afghanistan to capture Osama bin Laden was still unsuccessful and, to the Americans, embarrassing. Meanwhile American belligerence was losing support among Muslims everywhere, and leading to much soul-searching in the West itself. I found it hard to remember the extraordinary upsurge in sympathy for America of just a year earlier.

11.09.2002

WE CAN all recall what we were doing a year ago today, but can we recall what we were thinking? In the flash of crisis the mind instinctively marks the body's space, cloaking it with protective context. The mind gets no such help. It goes crazy.

I know what I thought because it appeared on this page last September 12. I reminded myself that I was more than "pro-American", that all my life I had loved the place and especially New York. My surge of horror was thus allied to a passionate sympathy. The gibes of some Europeans at America's "self-inflicted wound" seemed idiotic, sickening. Yes, Frankenstein was in a sense consumed by his own monster. But only the most worm-eaten and polluted morality could fail to damn this deed. The heart of darkness had come to the heart of light. It was unconscionably wrong.

I therefore prayed that America would not dignify a monstrous crime by making it a war. The power of terror lies not in the act but in the aftermath. Its multiplier effect thunders round the globe as publicity fuels insecurity. Surely, I thought, America was rich enough and confident enough to defy the terrorist by refusing to overreact to his challenge. The American way of life was at risk from such assault only if America made it so.

The same view was put by the hero of the hour, Rudolph Giuliani, the mayor of New York. He told his citizens to stay calm and go about their business, to "buy a pizza, take the kids to the park and see a show". They must not show fear or run for cover.

Mr Giuliani was cheered but ignored. Americans stopped buying, stayed at home and drove their economy into recession. Yet for three astonishing weeks, the world tore up its anti-American stereotype and declared whole-hearted sympathy. It was a golden moment. *Le Monde* declared that "we are all Americans now". Russia, China, Saudi Arabia, Egypt, Syria, Iran, Pakistan, and even one Taliban faction in Afghanistan promised to join the hunt for al-Qaeda. Suddenly to be anti-American was indeed to seem pro-terrorist.

These recollections now seemed far away. The age of intervention – gone into limbo before 9/11 – was now raging. On the anniversary of 9/11, George Bush gave an extraordinary speech to the UN. It was not a sad reflection on how the tragedy, albeit briefly, brought the world together against terrorism. It was a long, sustained rant against Saddam Hussein as a menace to world peace.

Saddam, said Bush, was harbouring terrorists, building chemical and nuclear weapons, threatening his neighbours and the world. "Tens of thousands of political opponents and ordinary citizens have been subjected to arbitrary arrest and imprisonment, summary execution and torture by beating and burning, electric shock, starvation, mutilation and rape." Warming to his theme, Bush added that "Wives are tortured in front of their husbands; children in the presence of their parents; and all of these horrors concealed from the world by the apparatus of a totalitarian state."

Every motive for intervention was tossed into the rhetorical pot, humanitarian, philanthropic, defensive, pre-emptive, democratic, "responsibility to protect". Bush demanded that the UN act to bring Saddam to heel, with the clear implication that if it did not then America would. It was a speech of remarkable belligerence.

13.09.2002

WHEN RUNNING for office George W. Bush was emphatic. As far as the world was concerned, he was opposed to adventurism and intervention. He said he wanted a "humble foreign policy". He told his opponent, Al Gore, that it was not America's job to "go around the world saying 'this is the way it's got to be'".

Yesterday at the United Nations he reversed this position. In a remarkable assertion of global sovereignty, he told the UN to get rid of President Saddam Hussein or he would do the job himself. He reinforced in meticulous terms his swelling crusade against evil. Though he paid due respect to the traditions of the UN, no quarter was given to such tenets of the postwar international settlement as national sovereignty, the sanctity of borders, or multilateral legitimacy and the rule of law. Saddam offered legitimacy enough.

Though Mr Bush presented no "killer evidence" of an imminent threat from Iraq, he defined Saddam as a time bomb waiting to explode. Arms inspectors seemed neither here nor there. Nor did Mr Bush give Saddam any bridge over which to retreat. He leaves the UN offering Saddam no reason for compromise, with nothing to lose.

I do not regard America as the Great Satan. I therefore do not regard Mr Bush's motives as an evil equal to that which he opposes. He may be alarming. His plan to bring democracy and peace to the Middle East may be unrealistic and the means dangerous. But an America that wishes to engage with the world to make it a freer and happier place cannot be bad. Unlike many, I do not doubt the sincerity of Mr Bush's motives. The moral thrust of yesterday's speech was reminiscent of the Indian summer of the British Empire. It was presumptuous, but not wrong.

Shortly after Mr Bush took office I wrote that he might prove a surprise. Texans were not ordinary Americans, they were extraordinary. Mr Bush was courteous, well-spoken, punctual, smart, extrovert in manner but introvert in family and friendship. He could be a natural spokesmen for Middle America, closer to the provincial directness of Ronald Reagan than the brash urbanity of Bill Clinton. Above all he was not naturally partisan. From the moment he arrived in Washington he sought concord and coalition.

So it has mostly proved. Tony Blair protests that the simpleton George Bush of caricature is "simply not the man I recognise". A Harvard MBA is hardly a dumb qualification. At present Washington is awash in presidential analysis. Bush is depicted as an intelligent man, not articulate in public but level-headed and good at man-management. He has gathered an experienced team whose diverse views he marshals with skill. His Administration is not a bunker but a seminar which, according to one insider, "is a lot more interesting and impassioned than the debate outside it".

Yet this debate has yielded an astonishing shift in ideology. Before September 11, 2001, Mr Bush's stance towards the "arc of instability" in the Middle East was clear. It was to respect Condoleezza Rice's (then) doctrine of neglect. It held that Israelis should find their own peace with the Palestinians. The Iraqi leader should be contained with bombing and sanctions. The al-Qaeda threat was recognised but ignored as the usual anti-American "noise". Foreign policy should be "soft".

After September 11, the stance evolved with startling speed. At first Mr Bush promised only to "hunt down and punish those responsible". Two weeks later he was "at war" against "every terrorist group of global reach". After Afghanistan and the military debacle of Tora Bora and Operation Anaconda, he did not retrench but sought new fields of intervention. Al-Qaeda was left to regroup in Pakistan, a country unmolested as a "friend" despite copious evidence that it was a terrorist haven.

The War on Terror went abstract. Foes were never named. Instead Mr Bush enunciated a wholly new doctrine of defence. At West Point in June, he specifically rejected the "cold war doctrines of deterrence and containment". America, if necessary acting alone, would "take the battle to the enemy, disrupt his plans and confront the worst threats before they emerge". Mr Bush openly claimed the right to pre-emptive aggression against any state that might threaten America, or its neighbours or even its own people. In this, as we saw yesterday, the UN might be a help but was not necessary. Mr Blair apparently agrees.

On 24 September 2002 Blair published his promised dossier claiming that Saddam was preparing weapons of mass destruction, including chemical and biological agents and long-range ballistic missiles. He was also acquiring material to make a nuclear bomb. This all constituted "a current and serious threat to the UK national interest". The document disclosed that Iraq's military planning "allows for some of the WMD to be ready within 45 minutes of an order to use them". Inaction against Saddam was "no longer an option", said Blair. Every one of the allegations made

in the dossier was later discredited by the coalition's post-invasion Iraq Survey Group.

Three weeks later, on 12 October, Islamist fundamentalists exploded a car bomb in the tourist district of Kuta on the Indonesian island of Bali. It killed 202 people, including 88 Australians, 38 Indonesians, 27 Britons, 7 Americans, 6 Swedes and 3 Danes. I examined what should be the nature of the response.

16.10.2002

WHAT AWFUL horror is now being hatched in some hotel room or garret? Yesterday the Foreign Office added its mite to global terror by telling British citizens to avoid poor Bali, which must now be as safe as anywhere on earth. London is far more at risk. At the same time Tony Blair told the House of Commons that the threat from "weapons of mass destruction" is as great as the threat from terrorism.

I find it hard to credit that Mr Blair really believes this. Even if it were true, no sensible person could hold that declaring war on Iraq is the best way of averting either threat. Over the past decade a gang of fanatics, financed by Saudis and trained mostly in Western cities, have tried to sow mayhem round the world. Occasionally they have succeeded. They have apparently not been caught.

People are being murdered now, not in two years' time "if Saddam were able to get some uranium from an African source". There is not a shred of evidence that President Saddam Hussein is behind any recent outrage. There is evidence that al-Qaeda is still active. Iraq must now be distracting every intelligence resource in the whole of Asia and recruiting hundreds to the militant cause.

Bali should stir a real argument over the containment of terrorism. The argument is over means, not ends. Peace-loving people everywhere want terrorism crushed. They want relations between states governed by tolerance. They do not agree on how.

The initial thesis is simple. It is that the growth of sophisticated terrorism can brook no compromise. The explosive force of September 11 has been repeated in less dramatic incidents in Yemen, Kuwait and Bali. States that house and train terrorists must be crushed. States that might do so in future must be crushed as well. America has the power. It must do the deed. This thesis holds that the United Nations concept of national sovereignty is defunct. Might grants America the right of entry, search and arrest. Even a putative threat, as in Mr Blair's Iraq dossier, justifies a pre-emptive attack. The War on Terror is, said George Bush a year ago, an all-out war, a world war, a war possibly without end.

Last month the thesis was restated in the White House's astonishing and little-noticed National Security Strategy. This asserted America's right to stop any other country "from pursuing a military build-up in hopes of surpassing or equalling the power of the United States". It also asserted America's generalised right to take pre-emptive action in support of that hegemony. The assertion acknowledged no external authority. Instead it required a large military budget – "full spectrum dominance" – because pre-emptive attack needed more power than mere deterrence.

The antithesis regards this thesis as dumb. It holds that terrorism is fuelled not by the warrior's zeal for territory but by a messianic yearning to give a bloody nose to the rich and powerful. Such resentment is encouraged rather than diminished by talk of war. Anti-Western sentiment has long underpinned Third World politics. It will do so as long as wealth coexists with poverty. But the terrorist's power lies in his capacity not to kill but to incite fear, to play on Western cowardice and paranoia.

This antithesis demands that America make itself loved, not feared. The terrorist should be treated as a criminal. The tank of envy in which he swims should be drained, not filled with the "blood of martyrs". Americans should show the confidence of the powerful, not the trigger-happy jumpiness of the vulnerable. Westerners may be hurt by al-Qaeda, but the West is not threatened. Those who flaunt their wealth to the world must expect occasional stabs of resentment. So, cries the antithesis, America stay at home. Stop trying to bully the world.

These were the two positions, thesis and antithesis, on which the age of intervention now turned. Might they achieve a synthesis? The

new year of 2003 was ominous as governments in London and Washington turned up the pressure on Saddam. He clearly appeared to be flouting the UN, playing cat and mouse with its weapons inspector, Hans Blix. But would the UN be the vehicle to bring him to heal, and on what evidence? And who really believed that he constituted a global threat, either from terrorism or from weapons of mass destruction? Intervention now showed no sign of a concern for humanitarianism, only a strange, mendacious yearning on the part of some senior Western leaders for war.

01.01.2003

THIS IS the year when Britons may be asked by their Government to go to war. Iraq is said to pose a threat so gross as to demand the ultimate sanction of "defensive aggression". So said Tony Blair yesterday. I have pondered these words a dozen times and still find them unreal.

Let us tread carefully. Exactly a year ago I was puzzling over a different war, in Afghanistan. That war had been presented as the only way to bring Osama bin Laden to justice after September 11. I thought it was a mistake. At a time when the whole Arab world was sympathetic to America, I was convinced by those who knew Afghanistan well that the best way of capturing bin Laden was through the Saudis and their friends, the Taliban. Exploit the sympathy for America. Put on the big squeeze and sooner or later bin Laden would be popped.

For America that proved a politically unrealistic response to September 11. The Saudis were ignored and the Taliban was toppled. The Afghans were freed from an oppressor, but bin Laden was not found and his al-Qaeda dispersed. Its operatives are said to be on the loose and anti-Americanism is on the rampage. But there was a sort of "victory". Someone had been punished for harbouring bin Laden.

This past year we have learnt that combating terrorism is the same messy, hit-and-miss business it has always been. Each weekend Downing Street and its "terrorism unit" summons the press for the Sunday scare story. We have now had the nine-eleven anniversary scare, the sarin-on-the-tube scare, the smallpox scare, the "threat to public transport" scare, the Christmas shopping scare and last Sunday's "London quarantine" scare. (Note, these stories always appear on a Sunday.) They offer no useable public advice. They are pure heebie-jeebie.

Despite the terrorising of American and British citizens by their governments, there is no apparent evidence that they are any more at risk than they have always been. For a quarter century, planes have been downed, bombs exploded and innocents killed. Baader Meinhof, Carlos the Jackal, the PLO, the Red Brigades, the IRA, killed and maimed their way across the 1970s and 1980s. All Europe has learnt to live with varying degrees of terror.

It is always possible that a fanatic is at this moment planning a new outrage. But there has been no repeat as uniquely dreadful as was September 11. The most serious attack, in Bali, was an old-fashioned car bomb. Other incidents may have been stopped by good detection and good luck. Given the level of defence expenditure, we are entitled to expect both. George Bush was right after September 11 to say that combating terrorism was "forever". But so should normal life be forever.

Of all the "paxes" the world has been offered in history Pax Americana is to be preferred. Its imperium is that of humanity's most successful melting pot, by most standards democratic, enterprising and free. After its lead role in the three great confrontations of the twentieth century, America has won its spurs. Yes, it would be wise to seek the support of the world community for its constabulary duties. But there may be times when that support is not forthcoming, and the duties required nonetheless.

These duties must imply a capacity for war. The Italian writer Umberto Eco, in his *Essay on War*, pleaded that "hot war" should by now be as taboo as incest. In future, he said, conflict should be cold, conducted by ceaseless negotiation and argument. Clausewitz should be reversed and politics become the pursuit of "war by other means". I regard this as a cop-out. Policing implies the threat of sanction and sanction implies its occasional activation. The Vietnam, Falklands and Gulf wars were all fought in a wider cause than that of national self-defence. All of them, to my mind, had "just cause".

Iraq at present is not in this category. It is not attacking or threatening a foreign state, though it must be perilously close to having "just cause" for self-defence. Britain's national security or political stability is not realistically in danger, however much Downing Street may try to scare us each week. Iraq is a nasty place and military planners must have contingencies. But to no one can Iraq be said to pose a sovereign threat sufficient to require a pre-emptive war.

That is not necessarily the end of the matter. What is ironic is that the best argument for an attack on Saddam is precisely the one against which the British and American Governments are trying to guard their flank. Iraq appears to have broken the UN's rules on what constitutes a legitimate arsenal for self-defence. The hiding and cheating must end or such rules become worthless. A man may deny his intention to use his unlicensed machinegun, but he will go to jail if he persistently will not surrender it.

These rules are United Nations rules, not American rules. It is the UN's authority which Saddam flouts. The purpose of any conflict would be to uphold that authority. If the rules are seen as merely a subset of American foreign policy, obedience to them will seem no more than obedience to America. The UN's authority will be doubly undermined.

If the UN is to authorise an attack on Iraq, it must be satisfied that its rules really are broken. It must know that Saddam is building up his nuclear and other arsenals. It must have intelligence from whatever source to show the world, especially the Arab world, that he continues to be a cheat and a menace. The UN must accept that containment has failed and that no means short of military conquest can achieve enforcement. Unless that condition is met, Saddam Hussein has broken no peace. There is no cause for Britain to go to war.

At this stage the world had only the evidence presented by intelligence agencies in London and Washington to guide its response to events. On 3 February 2003 this led to an apparently updated reissue by Blair's press secretary, Alastair Campbell, of the September dossier. It had already been dubbed "the dodgy dossier" and edited to buttress the case for war.

Dispassionate observers – and they included me – were left with little option but to accept the evidence as presented. We could not imagine what later emerged as the lies in the dodgy dossier. We had to accept the imperative that the UN somehow enforce its disarmament resolution, Resolution 1441. But questions persisted over the spin put on the dossier by Blair's office, and on the proportionality of America's expected response.

07.02.2003

IS THE ground starting to shift? The past two weeks have been miserable for peace-makers. The ability of the United Nations to curb the weapons arsenals of Iraq's leader, President Saddam Hussein, has been sorely questioned. The material presented to the UN by Colin Powell may be, much of it, old and circumstantial. There may have been no "smoking gun". But the doubts sown by Hans Blix last month have been confirmed. The fox is up to his old tricks. The world still has a problem with Saddam.

The peace party cannot take refuge in complaining about America's behaviour, however high-handed it may be. Washington dismisses the UN as a sideshow and sees Resolution 1441 as diplomacy for wimps. But the world community set its hand to a task last October, that of finally disarming Iraq of the world's nastiest weapons. That task was enshrined in Resolution 1441 and in Dr Blix's inspection process. Resolution 1441 was its bible and nothing else can claim legitimacy.

On Wednesday General Powell was careful not to question that legitimacy. He must be its last guarantor in Washington. But he questioned its efficacy. Saddam had flouted a deal reached under UN Resolution 687 (1991) that left him in power. He continued to develop chemical and biological weapons and to seek a nuclear capability. For all his promises, including to the UN last October, he has plainly treated inspection as a game of deception not co-operation. Within the terms of 1441, the burden of proof is no longer on the inspectors to find weapons, but on Saddam to show where they have gone.

This challenge was well set out by the Foreign Secretary, Jack Straw, in New York on Wednesday. The UN, he said, cannot constantly turn a blind eye to a breached resolution merely because each breach seems small and the threat not immediate. Unlike the oft-cited Israeli resolutions, this was not a request for parties to seek peace, but an order demanding it. Ten years is long enough to wait. The UN's credibility would be ruined by not responding.

This has nothing to do with al-Qaeda or Washington's desire for "regime change" or some notional threat to Britain or America. This is a collective decision of the UN. Honouring it is as crucial to its status as was Abyssinia to the interwar League of Nations. In 1935 Mr Straw's predecessor, Sir Samuel Hoare, boasted that Britain would be "second to none in its intention to fulfill the obligations which the Covenant lays on it". He promptly ratted on that obligation and had to resign. The Hoare-Laval pact still sends a shudder down the spine of every foreign secretary.

So far, so warlike. But ends have never justified means. In any military operation, other doctrines than rectitude and legality apply. One is the principle of proportionality. Another is the principle of unintended consequences.

The offence of which Saddam stands accused remains that of being a potential, not an actual, aggressor. No amount of fanciful espionage can get round this. While inspectors were in place in the 1990s, Iraq attacked nobody. After 1998, when Saddam lurched out of line, President Clinton unleashed Operation Desert Fox after Saddam's weapons stock, and thus his status as a potential threat, was declared "safely degraded". There is no shred of evidence that the stock is more of a threat today than in 1998, or that it cannot be likewise degraded.

This principle is enhanced by that of unintended consequences. I have read no coherent strategy for a benign outcome to this war. The war party clearly has no strategy for a defeated Iraq, except to leave British troops "for three years". It is careless of enticing thousands of suicide-bombers, warriors of a "free Baghdad", on to the streets of London and New York. This war will not end with the fall of Baghdad, any more than the war on al-Qaeda ended with the fall of Kabul.

Yes, there is a powerful case for enforcing Resolution 1441. Yes, Saddam presents the UN with a challenge of enforcement. But that does not justify the horror which British and American bombers are planning to unleash on the citizens of Iraq, and the vengeance we shall experience in return.

On 15 February 2003 global opposition to the impending American and British invasion of Iraq coalesced in a worldwide series of demonstrations, attracting between 6 and 10 million people in more than 600 cities. The *Guinness Book of Records* later declared it the largest such protest in human history. Meanwhile military preparations were underway for a massive air attack on Iraq – Operation Shock and Awe – followed by a land invasion from Kuwait. The age of intervention appeared to have gone berserk. I pondered the historical ironies of such a colossal conflict.

14.03.2003

THESE DAYS history mostly sleeps. But on Wednesday evening it leapt up, eyes staring, and screamed. It had just seen Tony Blair cruising into the Royal Academy to escort Gerhard Schröder, the German Chancellor, to the Dresden exhibition. The show is of 58 Old Masters from Germany left intact by the Royal Air Force in its firestorm of 13 February 1945.

Herr Schröder hardly needed this memorial to the horrors of aerial bombardment. He and his country understandably want no part in any repetition. Yet Mr Blair bade his guest farewell and returned to join military advisers in planning Operation Shock and Awe, the forthcoming two-day air blitz on Iraq. Among the weapons proposed is the new MOAB, the "massive ordnance air blast" or Mother Of All Bombs, revealed by the US this week. It could take out old Dresden in one blow. I cannot fault Mr Blair for irony.

The customary defence of the Dresden raid is that Britain cannot be to blame because German civilians deserved it. They deserved it for allowing Hitler to be their leader. The identical argument is now being deployed to defend the forthcoming rain of terror on Baghdad. However many people are killed and monuments destroyed, it can all be laid at Saddam Hussein's door. Victor's justice applies.

I find it astonishing that Britain must employ the Dresden defence to excuse anything at all. It implies that generals take their ethical lead not from their own rules of engagement but from the morals of the foe. This is absurd. It is also not how generals behave. Target lists are fiercely debated. Soldiers do apply moral standards to their behaviour in war. The limited military value of bombing cities is set against the political cost of so doing. Robin Neillands' recent analysis of *The Bomber War* contrasts the bomb as a tactical aid to ground troops with the so-called "strategic" bombing espoused by Harris's boss, Lord Portal, much to the latter's disadvantage.

The impending 48-hour blitz on Iraq – 800 cruise missiles and thousands of conventional bombs – will fall not just on people but also on the world's most vulnerable historic sites. History could hardly present a greater irony. Six thousand years ago, Mesopotamia saw the earliest manifestation of Western culture. It is now to see the latest. An estimated 10,000 archaeological sites remain, most as yet unexcavated. Many will now be excavated for the first and last time.

The destruction of cultural and religious monuments in war is explicitly prohibited by the Hague Convention (1954), which Britain and America refused to ratify for fear it might inhibit their air forces. The Sumerian city of Ur, dating back 6,000 years, was first revealed by the British archaeologist, Sir Leonard Woolley. Its great ziggurat and sacred court are now pitted with 400 shells from a misguided strafing and bombing raid by an American jet in 1991. They were intended for the nearby Tallil air-base, which the US afterwards protested should not have been sited so near the monument. The base was originally sited here not by Iraq, but by the British.

On 18 March the House of Commons debated going to war on Iraq, with a government majority in favour of 412 votes to 149. It is sometimes said that a sure sign of parliament in the wrong is when all sides agree. But with Blair playing the patriotism card, members felt under pressure to support the troops. Even so the number of government MPs who voted against the war was the most for over a century (indeed since the repeal of the corn laws).

A particular bone of contention was that, although the attack on Iraq fell within the general terms of a UN resolution, it had not been specifically authorised. Even the most determined of liberal interventionists searched in vain for a real motive for the war.

Three ministers resigned, including the former foreign secretary, then Leader of the House, Robin Cook.

19.03.2003

AS OF tomorrow, Britain will be at war with an Arab country that offers no threat to it or to anyone. British troops will be fighting an action which the UN would have declared unlawful if asked. Now we can only hope they win fast.

Yesterday the Prime Minister, Tony Blair, made one of the most impressive speeches in defence of foreign intervention I can recall. He gathered into his oratorical grasp September 11, al-Qaeda, Hitler, President Saddam Hussein and the deterrence of dictators in general. He admitted that the link between all these was "loose". But he was in full flight. He seemed galvanised by terrorism, mesmerised by weapons of mass destruction, obsessed with any and every chemical and biological threat. As for Iraq, the country was simply not to be tolerated. This was not the fireside-chat Mr Blair. It was the full Churchillian rig.

Mr Blair has been starkly unable to establish Saddam as a terrorist threat. He may have been exasperated by the UN Security Council's refusal to cow before his friends in Washington, but the fact is that despite fierce arm-twisting it did not cow. One reason was sheer American ineptitude in daily deriding the UN, its inspectors and anyone seeking peaceful disarmament. This swung world opinion against the much-desired "second resolution", boosting Saddam and undermining Mr Blair.

This destroyed the two pro-American coalitions forged after September 11, 2001 and again before last autumn's Resolution 1441. Both were real achievements of British diplomacy, and Washington's ham-fisted wrecking of them will rank among the fiascos of international relations. Small wonder Mr Blair shuddered after condemning France, when a backbencher referred to America's 75 vetoes on Middle East resolutions. Washington received hardly a mention in his speech. This was suddenly a very British war.

Now Pandora's box creaks open once again and out will jump the miseries, distempers and demons of war. We should remember what the ingenious Greeks left at the bottom of that box, a mistress called Hope. She did not escape. She remained "to assuage the lot of man".

Hope now pleads for a quick victory. Hope pleads for no gratuitous bombing. Hope craves a swift rebuilding of Iraq. Hope longs for the UN to pick itself up and play a full role in a reconstructed Middle East. Hope wants this war to purge once and for all America's September 11 trauma and rejoin the world community. Hope believes in America as a force for good in the world. Hope wants this war turned to good account. Hope hates the sound of bin Laden laughing.

6

Iraq: The Big One

On 19 March four large bombs were dropped on a farm outside Baghdad in an attempt to assassinate Saddam Hussein. The intelligence was faulty. He had not been there for months and others died in his place. Two nights later on 21 March the bombing campaign, characterised as "shock and awe", was unleashed on Baghdad and other cities, with 1,700 sorties and 504 cruise missiles. This was followed by a land invasion from Kuwait of 100,000. The Iraqi forces quickly retreated and Baghdad was captured by the first week in April. Saddam disappeared. But what should the occupiers do next?

09.04.2003

UNITED NATIONS, stay out of Iraq. Leave it alone. It is being conquered by America and Britain, and conquest is followed by either anarchy or military rule. Since the latter is preferable, a clear line of governing command must be installed, with a policing force at its disposal. Realpolitik demands that the Anglo-American coalition now take full responsibility for what it has unleashed. It must restore order and reconstruct this wretched country. The spoils of war must become the toils of peace.

As of last night, the military phase of the Iraqi adventure appeared to be coming to an end. Some thought that victory would be quicker, others thought that it would be slower. Nobody can be sorry that quicker won. Nobody could wish Saddam Hussein anything but dead. Western soldiers have done their job with the same brutal efficiency against lesser forces that once made the Roman legions unbeatable. But soldiering is straightforward. Now the politics begins.

Jack Kingston, an American congressman, spoke yesterday for many in his country when he laughed the UN out of court. It should "stick to cocktail parties and international gallivanting", he said, "and worry first about rebuilding itself". Americans had gone to war and won the right to determine the peace.

Let them. For all the emollient words of George Bush in Northern Ireland yesterday, those clearly deciding Washington's policy on Iraq hate the UN. They find it indecisive and wimpish. For six months, spin doctors have hurled at it the Big Lie, that the UN never grasped the nettle of Saddam Hussein. They ignore the fact that the UN did exactly what America and Britain told it to do, sanctioning and impoverishing Iraq in pursuit of their chosen policy of containment. At no point until the end did the Security Council deny Washington anything, even when most of its members rightly thought that bombing and sanctions were counterproductive to toppling Saddam. For Washington to accuse the UN of not grasping this nettle is outrageous.

Now that America and Britain have grasped it, they had better hold on to it. As Mr Kingston waves his Tomahawk over his head and cries, "Get lost, world", the world should retreat. Iraq will need ruling with a rod of iron. It will be a place awash with revenge squads, Sunni–Shi'a rivalry and gangsters fighting over reconstruction largesse. Such confederations need a strong central authority with armies to hold them together. Saddam and his Ba'athists were that. The coalition has destroyed such authority. It is inconceivable that it can be replaced in three months.

Once upon a time, British taxpayers might also have claimed reparation for the £3 billion they have spent pre-empting the "imminent and catastrophic threat" that Mr Blair told us Iraq posed to Britain. If this threat was real, sovereign compensation should be payable from Iraq's oil. If it was not real, who then should pay? War is never this tidy, but the new world order desires closure, as in Yugoslavia. The path to peace across the whole Middle East is now in thrall to American arms. In time that hegemony will seek legitimacy. It will seek it from the UN because it has the only legitimacy in town.

I have little doubt that America, so quick to go to war, will tire of peace when Saddam is gone and something else seizes the television screen. It tired of Afghanistan, even without Osama bin Laden being caught. In the Middle East its one commitment is to Israel, and that will not change, vastly complicating its rule of Iraq.

As occupation turns sour, Washington will see the UN as it did in 1991, not as a problem but as a solution, a dump truck on to which can be loaded the disposable refuse of military adventurism. Someone must guarantee Iraq's internal security when it starts to bore the Americans, or Iraqis will kill each other again.

Kofi Annan, the UN Secretary-General, should bide his time. He should say nothing and do nothing. He should sit in his office and let the used-car salesmen of empire come to him. They will offer him an old banger of a country, careless owner, badly dented. What would he need to take it off their hands? Then he can name his price.

On 9 April the statue of Saddam in central Baghdad was toppled and destroyed. America's victory appeared complete. But as the American secretary of state Colin Powell had warned, America now "owned" Iraq. What would it do with its new possession?

11.04.2003

VICTORY VALIDATES itself. Military triumph is so violent, so stunning, so photogenic that it brooks no dispute. Glory justifies price. A tyrant is crushed and for the moment a whole people is free. The toppling of Saddam Hussein's statue in Baghdad on Wednesday did not take 20 minutes or 20 days, but 12 years of Western misjudgment. But it is over. Thank Goodness that man is gone.

To what end? I suspect little will be heard now about weapons of mass destruction. This has been an exercise in toppling a hated foreign regime and hoping people will cheer. At present they will. Saddam's statue covered in the Stars and Stripes is war trophy enough. But if such a triumph is to be more than an act of ferocious gunboat diplomacy, America and Britain must convert it into an at least compliant region and an Iraq that is secure and free.

After the Falklands War, when the boot was on the other foot, I interviewed a Pentagon hawk who had been convinced that the

British would fail. He successfully advised that America deny ships or troops in support. In the event. I pointed out, Britain had won and Margaret Thatcher claimed to have deterred dictators from such aggression in future. The hawk laughed and replied that the Falklands proved only that countering aggression was dangerous and expensive. Aggressors would not be deterred.

He had been wrong about Britain but right in his scepticism towards deterrence. Russia duly invaded Afghanistan. Israel invaded Lebanon. Iraq invaded Kuwait. Milošević invaded Kosovo. They were not deterred, even after each in turn was worsted in subsequent war. If defeat deterred war, there would be no more war.

This war is different from Kuwait or Kosovo. It has involved the elimination of a country's entire leadership, public administration and system of justice. Those who traumatise a nation state cannot cut and run. Mr Bush cannot find a few symbolic "weapons of mass destruction", put his friend, Ahmad Chalabi, in an office block and vanish.

British troops in Basra yesterday protested that they could not ensure civil order as they "were not sent here to be policemen". But that is exactly why they were sent. They were to find and destroy weapons of mass destruction. They were to topple an evil regime. By force of arms they have asserted their authority in the streets of Basra. Surely they owe it to those they claim to "liberate" not to hand them over to the mobsters, looters and killers who ran Iraq before the Ba'ath party established ruthless order two decades ago.

The Americans and British say they have spent six months planning an interim administration for Iraq. Their armies have now established a bridgehead for this to proceed. Yet incredibly an interim leadership has not been agreed and London and Washington are said to be arguing still over the status of Mr Chalabi and the role of the UN. The search for a safe sheikh to "run Basra" is ominously reminiscent of Lawrence of Arabia's chaotic three-day rule of Damascus in 1918. He reluctantly concluded that "rebels, especially successful rebels, were of necessity bad subjects and worse governors". Iraq needs a long-term Western guarantee of civil order, even in the teeth of fierce local and regional opposition. That is the burden of this victory. Kipling called it the "savage war of peace". It must now be fought.

The lack of strategic motive for the Iraq intervention soon became apparent. Initially the objective was to find and eliminate Iraq's aggressive potential. That soon evaporated. Then it was humanitarian, to rescue the Iraqi people from a brutal dictator. Then it was political, to install a new democracy favourable to Israel and the West in oil-rich Mesopotamia.

These motives were soon obliterated by the sheer necessity of establishing order. As the Americans settled into the former Saddam compound, "the green zone", in central Baghdad increasing anarchy prevailed in the streets outside and in relations between the capital and Iraq's various provinces, now stripped of any governing authority. There was no appearance of law, or of any plans to impose it. I pondered the "nightmare scenarios".

23.04.2003

THIS WEEK the new Grand Vizier of Iraq, Jay Garner, landed in Baghdad and immediately declared his lack of legitimacy. "I am not the ruler of anything", he modestly announced. The only rulers of Iraq, he said, would be Iraqis. He did not say when.

At this moment, Iraq appears to be offered two if not three constitutions. One in the Kurdish north emerges from the barrel of a gun. It is nationalist and separatist. In the absence of a strong power in Baghdad, such separatism may yet provoke the intervention of Turkey and further war. Another is offered to the majority Shi'as in the south, a constitution of Sharia, of the Koran, the mosque and the burka. Then there is Sunni Baghdad, which may yet hope to become the Beirut of the region, but not if the ayatollahs control the army.

These are the "nightmare scenarios" of the US former envoy to Baghdad, Joseph Wilson. They envisage the seizing of power by Muslim fundamentalists, backed by armed militias emboldened by anarchy. They are unlikely to do America's bidding. They may be acceptable to Iraqis in the short term, as an alternative to anarchy. But they will not be democratic. Nor does experience suggest that they would be stable. General Garner will need all his skill to avert such a political collapse of Iraq. Collapse may not be the West's business, but stability and democracy were the promise of this exercise.

Americans now talk of withdrawing troops in a matter of months. That must terrify any putative Iraqi democrat. He will abandon all thought of standing for election. He will go to his mosque, say his prayers and grease his Kalashnikov.

On 1 May George Bush landed in a jet on the deck of USS *Abraham Lincoln* off the coast of California and declared Iraq a "mission accomplished". He was ecstatically received. It was the rhetorical high point of the age of intervention. Bush declared that, "Iraq is free. When Iraqi civilians looked into the faces of our service men and women they saw strength of kindness and good will ... the ageless appeal of human freedom. Everywhere that freedom stirs let tyrants fear."

The following week, on 12 May, massive car bombs exploded in three residential compounds in the Saudi capital of Riyadh, killing 39 people. Clearly Bush's mission had only just begun.

14.05.2003

THE BOMBS in Riyadh show that the threat of September 11 is not over. Equally clear is that the present danger is not from rogue states or weapons of mass destruction, but from murderous gangs with dynamite and cars. As Afghanistan was followed by Bali, so Iraq is followed by Riyadh. After waiting out the razzmatazz of war, reality terrorism is back in business.

These killers cannot be eradicated. Though they pose a threat to human lives they do not threaten Western values. They may stir dictatorial tendencies in paranoid politicians. But to imply that such incidents undermine freedom is to lose all faith in democracy. Whatever the motives, these are criminal acts. They should be met by the art of intelligence and the science of security, not by the crass hand of "regime change".

There will be no let-up in attacks without peace in the Middle East and an American and British withdrawal. That is a truism. But the job of security is not to solve the problems of the world. That is for politics. A policeman cannot end the grievances that foster violence. As Andrew Sinclair graphically remarks in his new book, *An Anatomy of Terror*, "a little learning is the nipple of the militant, when the mother's milk is hatred and revenge". The capacity of the West to generate hatred and revenge in the Muslim world is at present extraordinary.

Hatred festers in the bed-sits of North London as much as in the squatter camps of Arabia. Somewhere in a dirty souk or beneath a railway arch there will always be a maniac ready to pack a car with dynamite and drive it down the road to his – and my – death. I want that maniac in the souk stopped before, not after, he does me harm. Against him a billion pounds of bomber circling overhead and proclaiming regime change and freedom is no protection. He will be stopped only by another man in that souk, with a radio and a gun. Such protection offers politicians no glamour and contractors no profit. It wins no elections. I do not care. We have had the razzmatazz of war. Now let us have the reality of protection.

Two months after the invasion no sign had been found of Saddam or his weapons of mass destruction. Already questions were being asked of the robustness of the evidence for the war, and of the "dodgy dossiers" used by London to justify it. In particular Tony Blair seemed desperate to present the war as vital to protect Britain from attack, rather than protect Iraqis from Saddam Hussein. He wanted to play defence not humanitarianism. Yet again the age of intervention had at its core a central confusion of motives.

04.06.2003

HISTORIANS SHOULD note. At the turn of the twenty-first century Britain was ruled by two men, a lawyer and a tabloid journalist. The first profession does not do whole truths, the second does not do long sentences. Both suffer occupational hyperbole. Neither likes being wrong.

Now a third and nobler calling has crossed the path of Tony Blair and Alastair Campbell, that of spy. The head of Whitehall's Joint Intelligence Committee (JIC), John Scarlett was head of MI6's Moscow station and reputedly the last man in that city to wear spats. A person of some panache he, or at least his 'friends", were clearly driven beyond endurance by the antics of Messrs Blair and Campbell.

Last September Mr Scarlett found himself in that familiar bind of the intelligence assessor. His bosses were screaming for material "to cook", to justify a preconceived policy. They wanted evidence to support Britain in joining an American invasion of Iraq, should that come to pass. Every sinew was to be strained to find evidence of weapons of mass destruction (WMDs) posing an "immediate threat" to Britain. Any old tosh and gossip would do.

Mr Scarlett should have stuck to the holy writ of his profession. He should have pointed out that the integrity of intelligence depends on independence and judgment. Each prediction each nuance is exquisitely crafted. It cannot be "sexed up" or "put through Alastair's typewriter", like a tabloid front page. The assessor says, with Pontius Pilate, "What I have written, I have written."

With hindsight the JIC should indeed have gone down on its collective knee and pleaded with Downing Street to present Iraq as a humanitarian issue, not a "threat". It could have offered blood-curdling tales of torture death cells and mass graves. But that was not what Mr Blair and Mr Campbell wanted. Throughout 2002 they denied any policy of regime change. Aggression required evidence of urgency. They had to satisfy the Attorney-General, the Labour Party and the UN that Britain needed defending against Saddam Hussein. That is why Mr Campbell seized the JIC assessment and its raw material and, like a Fleet Street pro, took the best bits to the top of the story. I am told that the fell phrase "ready in 45 minutes" was not even in the assessment.

Mr Blair was adamant as recently as 23 March "that our aim has not been regime change". He abused the UN weapons inspectors, not for ignoring Saddam's torture chambers but for ignoring weapons of mass destruction "which I know are there". He curdled London's blood with "intelligence" of imminent chemical and biological attacks, even sending tanks to protect Heathrow from them. Nor has Mr Blair weakened in this commitment. His loyalty to Saddam's military might is worthy of Iraq's information minister. When even his mentor, Donald Rumsfeld, has given up on the weapons and withdrawn his search teams, Mr Blair keeps the faith.

On 8 July Blair appeared before the Commons liaison committee to explain his reason for invading Iraq. He cut a bizarre figure. He still intoned that somewhere there were Saddam's weapons of mass destruction. He was adamant that they existed and just had not yet been found. He seemed a little demented. Why not shift his tune and claim the invasion was all about regime change and being kind to Iraqis?

09.07.2003

IF NOT FOR the prime minister, the pretence that the weapons no longer matter and that real men shoot first and find lawyers afterwards. Mr Blair is a lawyer. For him Saddam's arsenals remain the *casus belli* in Iraq because that is what international law requires. They must exist. They do exist. They are fragments of the True Cross, sacred relics of Mr Blair's holy global empire. Believe in them and you shall be saved.

Accuse Mr Blair of claiming two plus two equals five and he will slay you. He was misheard ... five was just a ball park figure ... adding one to four is standard legal practice. He will protest that the Joint Intelligence Committee had double-sourced the five while both the twos were dodgy. A maths czar is in place and we should shut up until he reports. It is Mr Blair's belief, indeed his passionate conviction, that two plus two equals five. Anything else is frankly, honestly ... you know ... preposterous.

Mr Blair bought into sanctions against Iraq. He bought into containment. He bought into the bombing of Baghdad. He bought into the humiliation of UN weapons inspectors and the rush to war. He bought this much of the American ticket. Yet Mr Blair refuses to join America in holding that invasion needs no further legitimacy and its justification no proof. The prime minister is a legal perfectionist. He will make no Mother of All Apologies. There will be no "closure" on weapons of mass destruction. They will be found in Iraq if Hell has to freeze over first.

By September of 2003 Iraqi resistance to the American invasion was gaining strength. The occupation had already sent 500 body bags back to the United States and was costing American taxpayers a billion dollars a week. I wondered over historic parallels, other conflicts where initial ambition parted company with reality.

17.09.2003

I hear an echo. In 1919 Moscow's rulers were so exhilarated by the triumph of communism that they determined to bring its benefits to the outside world. This was to be led by Lenin's Communist Party under the leadership of the Comintern. Agents were dispatched and uprisings stirred wherever bourgeois oligarchy seemed ripe for toppling. Trotsky sat in his armoured train, fantasising that no force on Earth could withstand his revolutionary Red Army. The Comintern boss, Zinoviev, declared that all Europe would soon be one socialist state. Communist ideology followed where European crusaders and British imperial missionaries had formerly trod.

Within half a century some version of that ideology had overtaken half the globe. The *Internationale* won the hearts of liberal-minded people everywhere. The export of Russian communism must rank among the great disasters of human history. Its final demise in the 1990s was one of the great triumphs. But I shudder to see new crusaders for capitalism and democracy mimicking the attitudes of Trotsky and Zinoviev. Flushed with victory and blind to the views, or sovereignty, of others, they crisscross the Earth claiming the right to superimpose their order on its states.

The zest for world government is as old as Alexander the Great and Genghis Khan. Yet it cannot be soundly based when its chief enforcer, in this case America, regards any constitutional constraint as optional. The UN is humiliated. Treaties are ignored. International law applies to the weak but not the strong. Nobody accepts Kant's requirement of a moral dictum, that it must apply universally or it will enjoy neither consent nor deterrence.

Nation states are biting back. When democracy is allowed to speak, in Sweden over the euro or in France and Germany over Iraq, publics reject the automatic moral authority of supra-nationalism.

Across the Middle East, Western intervention has fuelled the ghoulish menace of suicide killings. The West regards itself as entitled to overrule the integrity of states once guarded by the UN charter, yet America and Britain display hypersensitivity when threatened in return. London today looks more embattled than it has since the Blitz.

I am not a pacifist, merely a realist. I regard greater humility and deference to the self-determination of states (however awful) as probably wise. Just as we are unlikely to change the world's climate, however many conferences we attend, so we are unlikely to impose our values on the Middle East, Asia or Africa, however many states we invade.

Peoples formed themselves into autonomous nations for a good reason. Nations expressed their affinity, their sense of belonging. The post-Cold War craze for supra-national action, to intervene at every opportunity to bring the world to order, has lost touch with national roots. It has lost its domestic accountability. Come back, Voltaire. We help the world best by tending our own garden.

In November 2003, six months after the invasion, I travelled to Baghdad to interview the new American head of the provisional administration, Paul Bremer. In Baghdad I was surprised by the state of the city we had so recently conquered.

07.11.2003

THIS CITY is not as I thought. Nowhere ever is. I have not been here before and can only compare it with other distressed cities. To outsiders the Iraqi capital is not a place but a giant question mark. Is it better, or is it worse? From the corkscrew flight path of the landing aircraft to the rubbish fires rising into the desert sky, Baghdad seems haloed with queries.

The city is bigger and more handsome than I expected. It has the spacious boulevards of dictatorship, but pleasantly tree-lined and planted with flowers. The poor suburbs are those of any Third World country, but the smart ones might almost be Milton Keynes. Sanctions are always kind to the rich. Baghdad has little of the tedious monumentalism of Stalinist East Europe, rather the Sixties ostentation of a banana republic.

Saddam created astonishing structures. The daring geometry of his parade ground would win a RIBA award. The stupendous al-Mansour mosque still stands three-quarters complete, bigger than St Paul's Cathedral. Even bigger was to be the adjacent Saddam mosque, intended as the largest place of worship on Earth. It is a giant folly, its arches and unfinished piers rising hundreds of feet into the desert sky, attended by four giant cranes. American helicopters huddle like pygmies round its base. This is pure Ozymandias.

On the bank of the Tigris stands the old British Embassy, to which the "liberating" British apparently dare not return. The graceful building decays into its garden while boats scurry across the river beneath its terrace. Next door is the secluded Arabic Music Centre, guarding its instruments from the surrounding anarchy. Across the river stands the ancient Mustansiriya College, claiming to be the oldest university in the world. This is a charming spot, in a city I could well come to love. The horizon from the hotel roof is still one of minarets, palms and eucalyptus trees.

But then cities survive anything. As Tolstoy said of Napoleon in Moscow, no invader can hold such a place in thrall for long. Sooner or later it goes back to its business. The markets, souks, bandits and smuggling mafiosi of Baghdad are up and running, free of all taxes and policing. What hell's teeth are being sown thereby only time will tell.

I have known many cities that have seen regime change, such as Saigon, Beirut, Berlin and Pretoria. In none of them did the incoming regime permit, indeed perpetrate, the destruction of the entire security and administrative apparatus of the capital city, with nothing to put in its place.

Much of the trouble is that the CPA [coalition provisional authority] operates under military rules which reduce to total absurdity the doctrine of "total force protection". It is as if Genghis Khan had been expected to invade Mesopotamia with the Health and Safety Executive round his neck. American servicemen abroad used to fraternise with those they liberated. In Iraq they do not dare. They are confined to massively fortified barracks.

The most prominent symbol of this syndrome is the extraordinary decision to house the CPA and its boss, Paul Bremer, in Saddam's own hated Republican Palace, covering a huge chunk of central Baghdad. It is as if Tony Blair had decided to curry favour with London by commandeering a site stretching from Tower Bridge to Lambeth Bridge along the South Bank. The massive forbidden palace encampment now extends to embrace adjacent office blocks and the al-Rashid hotel and has been made all but invisible behind a gigantic bomb-proof wall covered in razor wire. Officials cannot leave the palace without armour and bodyguards, and many never do. It makes the Kremlin seem like the shop around the corner.

Baghdad's citizens are not wholly stupid and deeply resent being treated as conquered subjects. Of course they welcomed the downfall of Saddam, though they constantly point out that the United States once backed him. But everyone I have met finds present American policy incomprehensible. As I listened to yet another tale of scared soldiers killing in cold blood, of homes invaded and wives humiliated by searches, of tanks crashing into uninsurable cars, I wondered if the unimaginable were happening. I wondered if some fiendish Pentagon theorists had decided after all that Saddam should be made to seem the lesser evil. They would give him back Baghdad and retreat to Kurdistan and the South. In Baghdad I do not wonder alone. America let him off the hook in 1991.

A visit to Abu Ghraib and the Sunni city of Fallujah left me wondering at American tactics in the occupation. Most notable was the heavy reliance on military firepower to win hearts and minds of local people. It certainly was winning them no friends in this heartland of the Sunni Iraqis. I wondered what horrors this folly would one day unleash on the occupying troops.

12.11.2003

AMERICAN F16s bombed "enemy" houses outside the Iraqi towns of Fallujah and Tikrit last weekend. The bombings were the first from the air since President Bush declared his mission in Iraq "accomplished" in May. They coincided with a visit by the

American military commander, General John Abizaid. His visit was to tell the opponents of the American occupation of Iraq that "we are prepared to get tough".

The sound of each of these weapons smashing into Iraqi soil will have been music to the ears of al-Qaeda, whatever murky allies it has in Iraq. Its ambition is to draw the Americans into what is already called the "Sharon option" of retaliatory strikes. The noise of such bombs is not music to the ears of the Coalition Provisional Authority, now virtually imprisoned in Saddam's palace in Baghdad.

Here lives a latter-day Lord Curzon, L. Paul Bremer III. He is neat, handsome, coolly cerebral and utterly committed to his cause, to ruling Iraq until the natives have proved themselves a bastion against world terrorism. The challenge for Mr Bremer is vast. An entire generation of Washington neo-conservatives may live or die with him.

Bombs do not help Mr Bremer, who was summoned back to Washington last night for emergency talks. As under the British Raj, it is hard to ignore the emerging tensions between the differing arms of the occupying power. The military seem to have remembered nothing about hearts and minds since Vietnam. The ruled are still the enemy. Sweets are delivered to children in tanks. Kit is threatening, helmets and body armour obligatory and with no words of courtesy. As for soldiers kicking down the bedroom doors of Arab women, that must have created a hundred martyrs for Islam.

In Baghdad on Monday I watched an Abram tank trying to patrol Saadun Street in rush hour. Rommel might as well have rumbled down Oxford Street in a Panzer. A car lay hideously crushed under its tracks, nearly killing the driver, while pedestrians screamed abuse at the soldier. These incidents echo round Iraq. They are stupid, shattering the welcome the Americans initially received.

Like many colonial administrators, Mr Bremer likes to style himself "a historian". Yet nowhere in the world can history have found an odder helmsman than this man in this gilded cage on the banks of the Tigris. He seems baffled by a people he rarely meets and cannot understand how they can be glad Saddam is gone and yet eager for his own departure. He complains that "I just don't buy that we are unpopular", but he dare not walk the streets to find out. I am beginning to feel sorry for Mr Bremer.

In my last days in Baghdad I tried to assess whether my opposition to the invasion had been overstated. Whatever the motives for the intervention, they were evolving over time. Bush was changing his tune from stamping out a threat to toppling a dictator and building a new nation. Might some good not come of the removal of Saddam and might the attempted introduction of Western values and Western aid eventually pay off?

14.11.2003

I HAVE now seen a country liberated from a tyrant and a start to repairing the damage of 12 years of failed aggression against Saddam Hussein. Security in Iraq is not worsening: for most Iraqis it is getting better, despite the media's concentration on body counts. Foreign troops are being killed in increasing numbers, but that is a different matter. So surely it was worth the effort? Does it not deserve the benefit of the doubt?

Last month George Bush made a speech I thought was of great significance. It was billed as reinforcing his determination to hold fast in Iraq, but went much further than that. Mr Bush said that "60 years of Western nations excusing and accommodating the lack of freedom in the Middle East did nothing to make us safe ... In the long run stability cannot be purchased at the expense of liberty." The policy espoused by his father, to leave people like Saddam in place, had to be rewritten: "A free Iraq will be a watershed event in the global democratic revolution."

This was sensational news from a country that had supported Galtieri, Pinochet and the Contras and tolerated dictatorships from Saudi Arabia to Uzbekistan. When running for office Mr Bush had declared that "America is not in the nation-building business" and did not want to see "the 82nd Airborne escorting kids to school". Now he was into nation-building with a vengeance. The very same 82nd Airborne is camped in the schools, usually seeking protection from the children's parents. Non-interventionists might shudder.

But in recognising past failure and championing true democracy, Mr Bush deserves applause.

So what is wrong in Iraq? What is wrong is that any such championship has been vitiated by its implementation. We need have no quarrel with Mr Bremer's efforts to get reconstruction going, nor with Washington's sudden desire to transfer power to a provisional authority. But there have been too many U-turns. Mr Bremer first wanted nothing to do with Iraqi politics until reconstruction was under way. Then he reluctantly installed former exiles as puppets on his Iraqi Governing Council. Then he criticised them. Now he needs them more than he dare say.

The Arab press this week has been full of helpful hints on how America might extricate itself from this mess. They range from vague invocations of the UN and the Arab League to pleas for a swift return of Saddam's army and Ba'athist regime, with America continuing to pay the bills. Everyone would like to be democratic, but just now they would prefer to be safe, the classic preamble to renewed dictatorship. Instead, they hear Colin Powell talking on Wednesday of needing to transfer power to Iraqis – currently code for chaos – to be "accelerated". To many Iraqis it sounds as if Washington wants to compress ten years of Vietnam into ten months of Iraq.

The conclusion can only be that, laudable though Mr Bush's goals may be, his executive arm just cannot deliver them. America is not good at peacekeeping or nation-building. Its soldiering is rule-based and insensitive. Its troops hate getting hurt, not because they are cowards but because their political masters – the voters – hate it even more. They rely on warlords in Afghanistan and burgeoning "force protection" mercenaries in Iraq. It is as if America had delegated winning the Arabs over to democracy to the good offices of Al Capone and Global Risk Strategies Inc.

In the south of Iraq outside Basra lies the territory of the Marsh Arabs, by repute the most cruelly treated of Saddam's Shi'a subjects. Surely they at least welcomed liberation from their hated oppressor? A visit into these ancient marshes was not easily undertaken. I was advised to hire four guards on the basis that "if you do not hire them

they will be the ones who kidnap you". In the end only two turned up. They were much needed.

17.11.2003

THE MARSH tribes occupy 6,000 square miles of the flood plain around the junction of the Tigris and Euphrates rivers. Recorded by the late Wilfred Thesiger in the 1950s, they now present the coalition with a conundrum. In the mid-1990s Saddam drained the marshes with his "mother of all canals". This destroyed the tribesmen's aquatic way of life and drove many to the slums of Basra. The coalition is now re-flooding the land with pumps. Has anyone asked the marsh Arabs?

Thesiger found a medieval idyll of watermen poling their way through the reeds and living off fish. The houses they built on islands in the water are astonishing. A *mudhif* is constructed of giant piers of bound reeds, curving upwards to form a horseshoe arch. A series of such arches form bays, as in a Gothic church, covered in reed matting. The houses are cool, flexible in the wind and easy to dismantle during floods. They offer the noblest vernacular architecture I have seen.

There was no way this could last. Thesiger wrote in 1958 that the *mudhifs* "will have vanished in 20 years, certainly 50" and that "soon the Marshes will probably be drained". The marshes lasted another quarter century and the *mudhifs* exist still. Saddam's intentions were part defensive – the marshes abut the contested Iranian border – and part political. The tribes are notoriously lawless. But he built schools and clinics for the dried-out villages. I visited them. The marsh Arabs use the canals to irrigate their new farms.

Driving west from al-Madina into the deep Marsh, I encountered nobody who wanted the flooding back. While I fully accept that this may not apply everywhere, for instance to the east of the Tigris, it is what I heard. The farmers produce maize and vegetables. They prefer the dry ground and tracks along the dykes. Though one wizened 97-year-old assured me that "every change I have seen in my life has been for the worse", his sons and grandsons disagreed. Prosperity had attracted the latter back from Basra. They wanted no return to the floods. There is now talk of the coalition pumps being sabotaged.

These people reminded me of the Nile inhabitants of Luxor, after the building of the Aswan Dam. Yes they had opposed it. Yes dictatorship had treated them appallingly and their traditional way of life had been ruined. But no, they did not want Western romantics to return them to the Middle Ages. The marsh Arabs I met had no wish to be a theme park for Thesiger groupies.

That said, they retain one quality that Thesiger would recognise, ferocity. Driving along a dyke I was stopped by the sound of shooting ahead. Men were running to huts for guns. Women were fighting each other viciously with sticks. We were told that the local Obada and Mshawsi families were in a blood feud over the killing of a man. We negotiated our escape past groups of scared and wretched desperados, fully demonstrating Thesiger's warning that: "No sheikh however powerful and no sayid however revered could finally settle a blood feud." The scene may have been romantic. It cannot have been the future.

7

Iraq: Aftermath Part One

Intervention cannot hope to be consequence-lite. Paul Bremer's dismantling of the Iraqi army left the way open for the formation of rival militias loyal to Iraq's territorial, ethnic and religious groupings. In order to extricate itself from the country, the coalition had to suppress these. Britain's "time limit" on occupation of three months had already been exceeded. There was not even an interim constitution on which a new regime might be based. Increasing lawlessness was making this task ever harder. I pondered the eventual division of Iraq into three parts, on the pattern of the West's division of Bosnia.

03.12.2003

THOSE WHO try to do the undoable must also think the unthinkable. American strategists in Iraq are contemplating what they have always denied, the search for a "strong man with a moustache" to stop the present rot. If the result is not democracy, so be it. If the result is the dismemberment of Iraq, so be it. Iraq has become a mess. There is only one priority, to "get out with dignity".

The 16 May order disbanding the Iraqi army created 400,000 enemies overnight and gave the Saddamists what they most needed, a sea of Sunni resentment in which to swim. The wild shooting habits and hearts-and-minds ineptitude of the 82nd Airborne and 4th Infantry did the rest. They supplied a stream of blood-feud assassins. For Iraqis this inept occupation has brought to life the Arab proverb, "Better 40 years of oppression than one day of anarchy."

Iraq has only ever been held together by brute force. Washington is grudgingly accepting the view that this is unlikely to change. A new leader is needed to prevent the place becoming a global magnet for what the Arabist historian, Bernard Lewis, calls "new causes for anger, new dreams of fulfillment, new tools of attack". This was, after all, the view that Washington took in the 1980s when it decided to support in power a certain Saddam Hussein.

The 60 per cent Shi'a majority, long oppressed by Saddam and his Sunnis, sees its hour as come. Its primary allegiance is to ayatollahs who, however moderate, require government to be based on Islamic law. Like all Iraqi politicians, these men are playing it slow at present. They are watching the chaotic mood swings in the Republican Palace fortress in Baghdad – and biding their time.

Mr Bremer has turned the Sunnis into a mass resistance movement, armed and desperate. They have no jobs or oil and increasingly see Saddam as their champion against Shi'a domination. Their underground Ba'ath party is a lethal saboteur of any new regime. Baghdad, once majority Shi'a but now heavily Sunni, could become another divided city, a place of nightly horror.

As for the Kurds in the North, they will allow no loss of the sovereignty they enjoyed under the "no-fly zone". Their current leader, Jalal Talabani, would support a Shi'a regime for a while. But any Shi'a decision, say on oil, with which the Kurds disagreed would be opposed. Many Kurds have dreamt of an independence which has never seemed closer than now. Sceptics are already talking of Kurdistan becoming America's "second Israel".

For the Americans to try policing such a confederation is inconceivable. To hold the Sunnis in subjugation to the Shi'as, to deter the Turks from oppressing the Kurds, to reassure the Saudis over an Iranian-backed Baghdad, would all require hundreds of thousands of troops in perpetual battle mode. It is not on.

Iraq seems more likely than ever to split three ways. Fragmentation has become the default mode of Western intervention. It was so in Yugoslavia. It is so in Afghanistan. America and Britain apparently cannot tolerate the power centres needed to keep disparate nations in order. We may no longer divide and rule, but we happily divide and debilitate.

If this was the Pentagon's strategy all along, it has been implemented in a funny way. But since realpolitik has overtaken idealism as Washington's ruling ethos, at least an orderly break-up of Iraq should be planned, not denied.

The gyrocompass of intervention was now going haywire. Over the course of 2003, Colonel Gaddafi's Libya accepted responsibility for sponsoring a number of terrorist outrages, including the Pan Am Lockerbie bombing. He declared his intention to join the War on Terror and renounce weapons of mass destruction (of which there is no evidence he had any). There was not the slightest sign of Gaddafi loosening his ruthless grip on internal dissent. Yet Tony Blair was delighted, sanctions were lifted and oil companies flocked to Tripoli. Gaddafi's family was welcomed to London and to LSE, and Blair accepted a much-publicised invitation to Gaddafi's "desert tent". Commentators were finding the West's interventionist ideology ever harder to follow.

11.02.2004

YOUR STARTER for ten. What is the difference between a sadistic oil-rich Arab dictator who must be backed and feted by the West, and a sadistic oil-rich Arab dictator who must be bombed and sanctioned into submission? Answer: none.

The lucky dictator in the 1980s was Saddam Hussein and today it is Colonel Muammar Gaddafi. In the 1980s the Americans and British were selling Saddam materials for his weapons systems. We knew he was massacring civilians with them. During that time American planes took off from British bases to assassinate Gaddafi in his Tripoli palace. The bombs proved no more accurate than a similar mission to kill Saddam in 2003. Dozens of civilians died, including one of Gaddafi's children, but not the target.

Had Gaddafi died in 1986, his death would have been hailed as a triumph against terrorism. Had Saddam been killed then, it would have been seen as a blow to stability in the Gulf region. Twenty years later neither Saddam nor Gaddafi had changed in their essentials. Both tyrants had aged and become less of a menace to the world. Gaddafi had stopped sponsoring terrorists. Saddam had let the UN destroy his weapons stockpiles. Both still killed their enemies, suppressed opposition and impoverished their peoples.

Yet now it is Saddam whose death is sought by the West and Gaddafi who is hailed by Tony Blair as "courageous and statesman-like". Yesterday Mr Blair welcomed the Libyan Foreign Minister to

London to ask when he might pay court to the great man in his desert tent. This may be stomach-turning to those who remember the Abu Nidal slayings, the Lockerbie bomb and Gaddafi's arming of the IRA. But, hey guys, this is politics 2004-style.

In a new book (*The Breaking of Nations: Order and Chaos in the Twenty-first Century*) the diplomatist, Robert Cooper, seeks to analyse this confusion. He sees an America freed from the constraints of the Cold War and hurling itself round the globe. Militarily aggressive, it finds new foes in terrorism and "failed states". Then, politically defensive, it dashes home and minds its hearth.

Europe meanwhile grows soft, preferring "to live in a world of law rather than one of power". It views America's readiness to take on the ills of the world sometimes with reassurance, sometimes with horror. Failed states, says Cooper, guard their identity more than their real self-interest. They thrill to have found ways of getting under America's skin. The Pentagon's coercion through "shock and awe" may be macho but it cannot deliver. Cooper holds that the increasingly pacifist states of Europe must learn to rearm themselves. America's umbrella will not last.

This is too gloomy for me. I think the Americans will be "beaten" in both Iraq and Afghanistan, leaving chaos worse confounded than before. But this was not inevitable. In occupying Japan after 1945, America took advice from anthropologists and historians. In Iraq it rejected all such advice and relied on blundering, heavy-handed security. It is proving a mistake. But at least Washington can see disaster coming. It is already beating the retreat.

Or so most observers thought at the time, reinforced by the capture of Saddam Hussein in December 2003. But as Iraq fell into increasing violence over the winter of 2003–4, I wondered what traditional concepts of war and peace had to say to the new "War on Terror", what of the balance between aggression and pacifism. Two new studies of military intervention offered a sort of answer.

02.04.2004

I AM no pacifist. I hate violence but I expect peace to come with order. I accept that heads may get broken on the way. But peace can only be the one famously described by Clausewitz: if there must be war, victory lies not in defeating an army but in securing the willing submission of a populace. Stability, not a passing triumph of arms, is the test.

So how to react to a ghoulish mob tearing Westerners apart in Fallujah or some Muslim preacher openly encouraging his followers to attack Western targets? What would Mahatma Gandhi have done if he saw a man walking into a crowd with a suicide bomb? Should I not use violence against such people, rather than prod aloft once more the broken dove of peace? No responsible government can leave things to the dove.

Aggression had to be repulsed in the Falklands and Kuwait. The powerful have an obligation to intervene where they can relieve suffering, as in Ethiopia, East Timor and Kosovo. Those interventions, if not always their methods, were justified reactions to natural or political disaster. Such wars pass the test.

Not so the War on Terror now declared against militant Islamic groups from Luton and Crawley to Chechnya, Palestine, Iraq and Indonesia. This is not a war between states. It is not, whatever headline writers imply, between faiths. Largely because of the West's intervention in Middle Eastern politics, it is between the West and a small network of lethal gangsters. Their claim to religious justification is as tenuous as was the medieval terror of Pope Innocent III.

World opposition to these terrorists was never greater than during September and October 2001, in the aftermath of 9/11. There was never a more opportune moment to mobilise peace against terror. Over the next two years that opportunity was blown. Today, support for jihadism against the West has never been greater, extending even to the playgrounds of suburban Britain. This reversal has been a fiasco of diplomacy.

The historian Hannah Arendt held that nations which resort too readily to violence end up by losing power. Violence breeds violence. The doctrine of punitive aggression and pre-emptive war espoused by George Bush and Tony Blair pandered to democracy's basest instinct, the violence instinct. Coupled with military overkill – "shock and awe" – it ensured that the West would fail the Clausewitz test.

Two provocative rejoinders to this policy appeared this week. One is *The Unconquerable World* by Jonathan Schell, a restatement of historical non-violence. To him it was not war that brought about the French Revolution or created the world's two largest democracies, America and India. It was logic and the negotiation of events. It was not a Bush/Blair "pre-emptive war" that achieved the overthrow of communism. It was patient confrontation. The bloodless transformation of Eastern Europe vindicated that policy.

Violence, to Schell, does not work. It is rather an easy response to a crisis by those with power. The American and British attack on Iraq, unjustified by law or self-defence, was rather a crude assertion of global power. It was unrelated to terrorism and has done nothing to stem it. Its continued slaughter only worsens international bitterness.

The other rejoinder is the Oscar-winning film, *The Fog of War*, an engrossing memoir by the former American defence secretary, Robert McNamara. He confesses that the 1945 fire-bombing of Tokyo would have been a war crime had America not won. In Vietnam he made mistake after mistake, often through ignorance, usually through refusing to admit that he was wrong. Elsewhere he has called the invasion of Iraq, "morally wrong, politically wrong, economically wrong". He pleads only for today to heed the mistakes of yesterday, which it rarely does.

McNamara's lessons, illustrated with vivid archive footage, require us to see foreigners as human, read their minds and histories and anticipate their responses to what we do to them. Violence should be an aid to persuasion, not an exemplary punishment. We should recognise that it rarely deters.

I am not as sanguine as Schell that "constructive engagement" can always protect me against the world's monsters. Only force would have driven Saddam from Kuwait or Galtieri from Port Stanley. Only the disciplined deployment of nuclear weapons against the Soviet Union was likely to induce mutual disarmament. The price of peace is vigilance.

Where I agree with Schell and McNamara is in remembering that it is peace we are supposed to be buying. It is not fear or hegemony or "showing Arabs who is boss". Mr Bush's pre-invasion scrapping of Colin Powell's plan for Iraqi reconstruction and opting for Donald

Rumsfeld's brutalism turned the chance of victory into the certainty of defeat. Mr Blair's compliance in this grotesque mistake was shocking. Nemesis may yet come to the streets of London.

Books on the Iraq War now began tumbling from American presses, few of them flattering of the coalition's leadership. Rarely had a conflict received such instant analysis, or leaders been found so afflicted by "cognitive dissonance". There was now no celebration of "mission accomplished", rather a Western leadership apologetic and defensive. In Britain the Hutton Inquiry into the "dodgy dossier" and the death of a government scientist, David Kelly, reported in January 2004, ludicrously clearing the government of all wrongdoing.

23.04.2004

NEVER UNDERESTIMATE the power of a book. This week the veteran Watergate reporter, Bob Woodward, electrified the American presidential campaign with *Plan of Attack*, an intimate account of the run-up to last year's invasion of Iraq. Within 24 hours of publication on Tuesday, a parade of top administration officials, including Colin Powell and Donald Rumsfeld, rushed out responses. The Democratic challenger John Kerry mentioned the book at least twice in every speech. No chat show was complete without a plug. Two current congressional hearings on Iraq are awash with its revelations.

The potency of *Plan of Attack* comes from the fact that Woodward not only interviewed George Bush himself but had him encourage his Cabinet colleagues to talk too. When Dick Cheney or Donald Rumsfeld balked, Woodward blithely reminded them that "the President wants this". Mr Bush's aides are even promoting the book as good for their boss's image as a man of "prudence and resolve". To all of them a book seemed safe, almost discreet. That medieval means of communication, black ink on dead trees, was still history's most authentic vehicle.

Woodward's thesis is that Mr Bush was always determined to get rid of Saddam Hussein. The only questions were of timing and presentation. Hence the "fevered" antics of the Vice-President, Dick

Cheney, playing Rasputin to Mr Bush's ingenue tsar. Hence the massive distortion and pollution of intelligence in America and Britain. Hence the diversion of $700 million from Afghanistan to Iraq without telling Congress. Hence the "refrigeration" of Colin Powell, to whom sections of the Pentagon were "the Gestapo". Hence a deal with the Saudis to keep oil prices high until just before November's election. Hence the offer to Tony Blair to keep British troops out of Iraq, to shield him from his Labour foes.

The story is of obsession overwhelming argument and reason in the highest reaches of power. I find the indiscretion in high places amazing. It is as if the entire US Administration had forgotten their "victory" in toppling Saddam and now saw nemesis scything towards them. They were desperate to rebut history in advance. They emerge as rivals feuding while their mission lies incomplete and while soldiers are still dying on the battlefield. Each participant has his script. War must now vindicate history, not history war.

Woodward's book is not alone. His account can be crosschecked with a groaning cliff of Iraq books at the door of every bookstore. Richard Clarke's riveting *Against All Enemies* tells of Mr Bush's lack of interest in al-Qaeda before 9/11, and for a year afterwards. Mr Bush's former Treasury Secretary, Paul O'Neill, also describes the Iraq obsession in *The Price of Loyalty*. President Nixon's aide, John Dean, pitches in with a diatribe against the Bush cult of cabalism, *Worse than Watergate*. The fabrication of Iraqi weapons intelligence is related again and again in Hans Blix's *Disarming Iraq*, in John Prados's *Hoodwinked: the Documents that Reveal How Bush Sold Us a War* and in *The Politics of Truth* by Joseph Wilson.

The combined blast of these books makes Britain's Hutton Inquiry look like a peashooter. Most illustrate our old friend, "cognitive dissonance", the disease of leaders craving intelligence that supports their agenda and eventually getting it. CIA agents are ordered to "find" evidence of WMD or "lose your job". Mobile labs, launcher trucks, aluminium tubes, anthrax phials and unmanned drones soon take on the iconic status of Watergate's safes, tapes and break-ins. A dud invoice on some Niger yellowcake becomes proof that "he can nuke us in a year". A smoking gun in one draft is a mushroom cloud in the next.

British intelligence goes wild. While the Pentagon was passing unassessed raw material to the White House from the dodgy Iraqi National Congress, M16 was recklessly giving Downing Street raw material from the rival Iraqi National Accord. This was the source of Mr Blair's much-vaunted "45 minutes" claim, which appalled even the CIA.

Had everything run to plan none of this might matter. By now contented Iraqis were meant to be sitting outside the al-Rashid Hotel, toasting George Bush and Ariel Sharon in mint tea and reading *The Wall Street Journal*. Mr Bush's Cabinet colleagues were supposed to be penning victory memoirs, not appearing shaken before congressional committees, let alone plea-bargaining with history via the likes of Mr Woodward. We all know victory has a thousand fathers and defeat is an orphan. But rarely has defeat's path to the orphanage been plotted before the birth.

The anniversary of the invasion of Iraq found Britain's Labour Party not in joyous reflection of a "liberal" intervention well completed. It was in an ideological torment that seemed to mock the principles of its founding fathers. The certainties of the humanitarian urge passed it by. As the governing party at war it had to defend war, yet it lacked the conviction of war's motives. The confusions of the age of intervention numbed it into silence. And still the news from Iraq was getting ever worse.

12.05.2004

NEVER IN modern history has Britain been so humiliatingly in thrall to an overseas power as London now is to Washington. Ministers live in daily terror of news from the front. They squirm, prevaricate, lie and pray for release. The Cabinet could as well be hooded and piled in a naked heap while a jeering GI looks on.

Mr Blair's colleagues seem decent enough. They pop into parties, nurse a glass of chardonnay, chat about Arsenal and ask after other people's children. They are shocked by a Camden burglary or an Upper Street mugging. Yet Amnesty and the International Committee of the Red Cross (ICRC) indicate that, since last year, ministers have been collectively responsible for outrages reminiscent of the days of the Indian Mutiny. These include the bombing and shelling of civilian targets, revenge attacks on towns, beatings and the "routine" use of torture, and holding some 15,000 mostly innocent civilians in what amount to concentration camps. Are these the same right-thinking, liberal people we see nightly on our TV screens?

Nothing has demonstrated Mr Blair's emasculation of British political institutions so completely as Iraq. The Tories were already out of commission. They have supported every palaeo-imperial dispatch of British troops for half a century. What is astonishing is the silence of the Labour party. Old Labour would be raising hell today. Where today are the heirs of Hardie and Lansbury, Bevan and Castle? Where are the veterans of Suez and CND? The decolonisers are gone, as are those who held Wilson's feet to the fire over Vietnam. As Sir Thomas More said, *qui tacet consentire videtur*. He who is silent is seen to consent.

The collapse of collective government under Mr Blair has enabled presumably worried ministers such as Gordon Brown, Patricia Hewitt, Paul Boateng, Alistair Darling, Tessa Jowell and others to sit on their consciences over Iraq. They can say, "It's not my department." Yet they cannot dodge collective responsibility. They cannot pick the pie of moral cherries and spit out the ones that taste American. MPs are like Chesterton's dock-workers, whose "heart is in their boots./They go to hell like lambs, they do, because the hooter hoots."

Old Labour might have been antediluvian but its politicians were men of principle. New Labour politicians are men of place. Old Labour spoke its mind. New Labour speaks its text message. It was always in Mr Blair's pocket. Now it is in Mr Bush's. What a comedown.

By May 2004 the mightiest army put into the field since Vietnam and the most sophisticated military technology on earth had still not found Osama bin Laden. Where was he? I wondered how he might have been celebrating the anniversary.

19.05.2004

SOMEWHERE IN a cave on the Afghan/Pakistan border, a haggard man with a long black beard chalks a list of scalps on the wall.

He gives an occasional whoop of delight. Each day's news fills his eyes with tears of joy.

The mountain hideout of Osama bin Laden must be Exhibit A in any history of the early twenty-first century. Its victims now range far wider than the twin towers and the Pentagon. They include the hated Saddam Hussein and his Ba'athist infidels, the government of Spain, the Geneva Convention, the authority of the United Nations and the editor of the *Daily Mirror*. They embrace *habeas corpus* and the Chairman of the BBC.

When the current madness passes, Osama bin Laden will prove to have been no more than a pin-prick on the arm of the Terminator. His devastating impact was the result not of his Wahhabi genius but of American power, hijacked by a neoconservative Washington cabal and then "leveraged" by al-Qaeda terrorists. Thus does a lightweight judo player use the power of a much larger opponent to engineer his fall.

But bin Laden will have served a purpose. He will have shown how thin is the protective shield that guards Western nations from panic. He will have shown how easy it is to goad weak politicians into counter-productive wars against pathetic nations. He will have shown how fragile are the liberties that the West boasts it will require of subject nations. The Patriot Act, Guantanamo, Abu Ghraib and Labour's endless terrorism acts will be remembered long after the troops have departed Iraq.

8

Iraq: Aftermath Goes Steady State

By June 2004 the coalition's interim Iraq constitution was delivering an interim governing council. This was pending the election of a formal constitutional council the following year. It represented all sections of Iraq's political community and was designed to enable America and Britain to declare completion and depart. I was not alone in assuming this marked the end of the year-long intervention. What I wrote then now reads as unreal.

11.06.2004

GOODBYE IRAQ. Farewell from the front pages. You have infuriated, exhilarated and exasperated us for 18 months, but this is the moment for parting. For the second time in a year, George Bush and Tony Blair have declared "mission accomplished" and a "victory for the Iraqi people". Another group of local people has been told to pretend to run the place. Whether this is triumph or cut-and-run, who cares? One of the briefest and bloodiest chapters of modern Western hegemony is clearly coming to an end.

Relief and euphoria continue to emanate from coalition leaders at the G8 summit on Sea Island, Georgia. To secure Tuesday's UN resolution on the new Baghdad settlement, American negotiators conceded to all sides. The new Iraqi government has a "right of veto" over coalition activities. It has everyone's blessing and the usual promises of aid and affection.

Was anything so astonishing? Law and order is collapsing across Iraq south of the Kurdish border. Coalition Provisional Authority (CPA) offices are having to move into military bases before closing at the end of the month. American troops are retreating to barracks. Small wonder Washington has lost the will to argue. If Iraq's new rulers want America out, then America will go, gladly in the view of its soldiers. I would be surprised if any foreign troops are actively engaged in Iraq a year from now.

No less unreal is what I wrote two weeks later.

30.06.2004

THE MAGNIFICENT two, George W. Bush and Tony Blair, had promised to stay in Iraq "until the job is done". It is not done, but they are going. The coalition boss in Baghdad, Paul Bremer, dared not leave with head high, banners flying, populace cheering. He did not even leave by road. Very likely he would have been shot.

The coalition skulks out of Iraq as the Americans did out of Vietnam, in armoured helicopters, while another three-hour power cut leaves Baghdad sweltering and fearful. Pentagon apologists jeered: "Why not celebrate the good things in free and stable Iraq?" The answer is now clear. If Iraq were free and stable, nothing would have kept a certain president and a certain prime minister from flying down from Istanbul (as close to Iraq as they got) to say so. They did not dare.

The coalition's final decision, to get out early, was probably its shrewdest. Security in Iraq was worsening and nothing but corpses were to be gained by staying. True, 160,000 troops remain but they are increasingly confined to base. With the US presidential election approaching, the body bags are talking. The loss of 40 Marines in the May retreat from Fallujah was the last straw. A land which a conqueror cannot hold, said Clausewitz, has not been conquered. Discretion is the better part of valour.

Towns such as Najaf, Karbala, Ramadi and Fallujah, and Sadr City in Baghdad are now in the hands of gangsters and militias. The Kurdish region is beyond Baghdad's aegis. More important, so are the transport network, the highways and airports. Contractors have recently had to stop most infrastructure work, leading to a return of power cuts and oil losses. The stuffing has gone out of this intervention. Everyone, not just the Iraqis, wants "foreign troops out".

It insults the daily experience of Iraqis to call their anarchy freedom and their insecurity democracy. At this point, the grammar of the Iraq debate goes haywire. Verbs slide from present and future to past exonerative and future aspirational. We are told that yes, everyone knows mistakes were made ... (mistakes are always passive). We should set aside the past ... what Baghdad now needs is ... what all good people must hope is ...

We can all do hope. It is dead easy. I can hope that that nice, tough Iyad Allawi gains swift control of his country. I can hope his police assert control over the gangsters now ruling his streets. I can hope the Kurds accept rule from suspect Baghdad. I can hope peaceful elections take place next year "as planned". I can even hope that Dr Allawi one day dies safe in his bed. For cutting and running now read hoping and running. It leaves no trace.

In the event, the Americans and British did not leave Iraq in 2004. They emphatically stayed. Meanwhile the age of intervention was demanding their attention in Sudan. Its government was waging war against the non-Arab inhabitants of the province of Darfur. This had led to the massacre of hundreds of thousands of people and the displacement into neighbouring Chad of many more. The disaster was creeping onto the front pages. What could be a clearer summons to humanitarian intervention? This was ethnic cleansing Kosovo-plus. Surely common humanity demanded that something be done?

28.07.2004

SO WHAT do we do about Sudan? I mean really do, not just pose. Do we scold it? Do we condemn it, sanction it, threaten it, bomb it, invade it? Do we impose "democracy and prosperity" on Sudan, given that it badly needs both?

A year ago I wrote wondering why we were invading Iraq when Sudan might reasonably claim prior attention. Everyone except Tony Blair knew that Iraq was no immediate threat. Yet nothing was as nasty as the regime in Khartoum. Eighteen months ago news media were already buzzing with religious massacres, ethnic expulsions, starvation, rape and pillage in Sudan. Refugee camps were growing in Chad. So what was urgent about one murderous Muslim desert state, that was not urgent about another?

The answer was that there were no television cameras in Sudan. There was no oil. The regime in Khartoum was being "helpful" over al-Qaeda and its dying citizens were, quite frankly, black. Besides, today's Hercules can cleanse only one Aegean stable at a time. Sorry, Sudan, but your genocide would have to wait.

Now at last the cameras are turning their lenses on to the grim wadis of the Sahara. Presenters are learning to pronounce Janjawid, Omar al-Bashir and the odious Musa Khaber. They are dusting off the adjectives of atrocity and incanting the pornography of rape. The language of righteous indignation is always prelude to "something must be done". The aid minister, Hilary Benn, has arrived and declared a humanitarian disaster which, to use the Foreign Office's favourite epithet, is "unacceptable".

The humanitarian urge is not just commendable but a righteous spur to action. The needs of the Darfur refugees are no different from those of the Ethiopians in the 1980s or the Rwandans in the 1990s. They need food and tents, water and trucks, medicine and drugs, and an army of philanthropic young to distribute and administer them. These disasters may be the result of natural catastrophe or political conflict. But charity should be blind to the difference if it is to be impartial and effective. That was the charitable instinct that drove Henri Dunant in founding the Red Cross at Solferino in 1859.

The current tendency is to conclude that because much suffering is political in origin, so too should be the response. Macho intervention goes for the root cause, leaving wimps to look after women and children. But when outsiders to a country decide to relieve its suffering by meddling in its politics they seldom make things better. Those who bring charity at the point of a gun usually bring more guns.

Sudan did indeed see a massive charitable intervention, with refugee camps in Chad and elsewhere, but there was to be no military component. To that extent it was in my view a properly

humanitarian response to a local catastrophe. To liberal interventionists, however, the world was "standing idly by". Now nothing was going to save Darfur from civil war, which has dragged on ever since, killing a reported half million and displacing over three million. But Sudan, of course, was in Africa.

Besides, the West had other concerns, notably a presidential election in America, becoming a de facto referendum on Iraq and on George Bush's conduct of the war. To outsiders the campaign was no victory rally. Watching it on the east coast and in the mid-West I found it surprisingly bitter. It showed how poison can enter domestic politics when a distant intervention starts to go wrong and no one can see a way out.

30.10.2004

AMERICAN ELECTIONS are real. They do not echo, they choose. To hell with parties, platforms and manifestos, these events go straight to the heart of democratic leadership, collective trust in an individual. Small wonder they draw blood.

Nothing in my political experience has been as gripping as the Bush/Kerry contest. It has God and the Devil, charm and malice, wit and vulgarity – and is wholly unpredictable. For a brief moment the coliseum is emptied of clutter and two men fight alone, with the mob to decide on death or glory. The hatred between the two camps is now visceral. On television, in offices, coffee bars and dinner parties, men and women shake with rage at the antics of their foes. Media bias is outrageous: "Vote Kerry, Get Nuked", runs a headline. Election night parties have been advised to have therapists on call.

The Bush camp has made not just "liberal" but "Massachusetts" terms of abuse. John Kerry is depicted as an "anti-life" Satan, lacking consistency, principle and "the vision thing". He and his wooden-faced East Coasters inhabit a "reality-based community", at odds with Mr Bush's "faith-based" politics of instinct. Mr Kerry lacks a sense of the great American myth – myth here being a benign term – and of the nation's "historic narrative" in the fight of good with evil. Britons find this the language of a different political planet.

Democrats reply in similar terms. To them Mr. Bush is a crazed revivalist preacher. He has betrayed the American compact that statesmen should make people feel good. He makes them feel bad, scared, frightened in their homes and ready to splurge another $40 billion on defence. To the Kerry camp the President is guilty of intellectual treachery, displaying open contempt for rational, evidence-based argument. He simply lies. To the Democrats here is a man guided by prayer not reason, by biblical exegesis not the dialectic of modern government.

This is the first election for decades that has not been "about the economy, stupid". This campaign is about the will-o'-the-wisps, fear, insecurity and its antithesis, pre-emptive aggression. A Bush advertisement has wolves loping out of the forest towards the camera while a voice intones "weakness attracts those who are waiting to do America harm". This is a Hallowe'en election. "Alone in the booth ..." says another spine-chilling Bush ad, "Why take the risk?"

The neo-con strategy may seem absurd, changing from crisis to crisis. But its purpose is simple, to redefine America in ideological, if not theological, terms. Neo-conservatism is not a pragmatic response to the new world order. It is the crucible of a new America, with insecurity as its binding myth and 9/11 as its "reality check". Iraq could be anywhere. Hence a terminology of a fear so cosmic that the end justifies any means, however illegal or gruesome.

That November Bush was duly re-elected. This would soon be followed by a crucial election in Iraq to a new National Assembly, charged with writing a new Iraqi constitution and running the country pending that outcome. With continuing unrest threatening the election, coalition forces felt unable to withdraw. Mission creep was becoming mission entrapment. Yet Iraq still seemed to be placed on the back-burner, a cleaning-up operation, a messy exercise in state reconstruction.

19.01.2005

DON'T LET them distract you. There is only one election that matters at present and it takes place next week somewhere you may have forgotten, Iraq. Prime ministers may sun themselves in Egypt and chancellors kiss babies in Kenya. But there is still a war on, our war. Next week is supposed to be the beginning of its end.

For once on this subject I agree with the British and American governments. The election must take place. Postponement, as advocated by Sunnis and sceptics, would be disastrous, a blatant surrender to terror. It would undermine the Shi'a moderates and leave Iraq politics in limbo. Hundreds of Iraqis and dozens of British and American troops will die staging this election. Deaths are now running higher than at any time since the start of the occupation. Yet any way out of the present anarchy requires some political momentum. The one cause that the West can champion among Middle Eastern rulers is that people like voting.

The Iraqi election will be conducted under foreign guns, with closed borders, a curfew and no secure inspection. Voters are being asked to choose parties for a 275-seat constituent assembly to draw up a new constitution. This must happen. The last legal justification for the 2003 invasion, Iraq's threat to the West, evaporated last week with the disbanding of the weapons survey group. Next week's election is the only excuse Britain has for remaining on Iraqi soil.

When it is over we should get out fast. Sound policy should be based not on pious hope but on realistic analysis. The Government has been piously hoping for 18 months. It has hoped that Iraqis would find a government with sufficient authority to restore security. It now hopes that the catharsis of democracy will lead 250,000 "terrorists" – the latest CIA estimate – to lay down their arms. It hopes against hope that Iraqi forces will regain control of towns and villages from bandits and militias. Nor is this just a hope, it is a plan. Indeed it is the coalition's only plan.

In March there erupted in London a sudden sideshow over the legality of the Iraq intervention. This had long been a largely private debate within the legal community and the UN. Now a leak from a Foreign Office whistle-blower showed it had concerned many within the administration. Was the war legal? What had been the secret advice given to the cabinet by the British attorney-general, Lord Goldsmith, reportedly after the chiefs of staff had refused to

fight any war that might put them outside international law? Liberal intervention might be controversial, but surely it could not be illegal?

25.03.2005

THE TRUEST remark about the legality of the Iraq invasion was made before it began by the American president, George W. Bush. Asked if he was worried about international law, he is said to have replied: "International law? I leave that to my lawyers." Tony Blair does likewise.

So why the fuss over the mess in which the attorney-general, Lord Goldsmith, now finds himself? He is a lawyer working for Mr Blair as a government minister. At a crucial point before the invasion of Iraq, duty required him to change his mind. He changed it. Whether, as friends protest, he did so "genuinely, independently and with integrity" is not at issue. He changed it. As long as he refuses to say why, he must carry about the ball and chain of suspicion as to his motives.

Yesterday's leak of the uncensored resignation letter of Elizabeth Wilmshurst, the Foreign Office lawyer, leaves no doubt as to events. Throughout the winter of 2002-3 the view of government lawyers generally was that a further United Nations resolution was needed for an invasion to be lawful. Otherwise, as Ms Wilmshurst said, it would be a "crime of aggression". Saddam Hussein was "in material breach" of Resolution 1441, albeit according to dud intelligence. He was thus vulnerable to "necessary measures". But authority to take those measures lay with the UN Security Council, not No 10.

This opinion underwent a dramatic change after a visit by the attorney-general himself to Washington, where lawyers reportedly "sorted him out". A long unpublished paper on 7 March suggested that a second resolution might not be vital but would still be safer. When a resolution was not forthcoming, the attorney-general paid another visit, this time to Downing Street to see two Blair aides, Baroness Morgan of Huyton and Lord Falconer of Thoroton. Mr Blair was now on the brink of war and desperate. On 17 March a legal statement was duly made to Cabinet and read out in parliament stating the view that the invasion was fine.

International lawyers were overwhelmingly hostile to the Iraq invasion. There was only one apparently independent voice cheerleading for Downing Street, Christopher Greenwood of the LSE. Last week it was revealed that he had received more than £50,000 for his services from Lord Goldsmith, a fact never revealed in his media appearances. So much for academic independence.

I recalled that Anthony Eden had the same trouble with unhelpful legal advice prior to the Suez expedition of 1956. He too had effectively disregarded it. The reference to Suez was revived with the publication in the spring of 2005 of the Eisenhower–Eden correspondence during Suez. The parallels between the two interventions were fascinating, not least because roles were reversed: Britain was then gung-ho and America strongly sceptical.

22.04.2005

CONSIDER THE following. A British prime minister is so obsessed by a Middle East dictator that he screams "I want him destroyed" and declares war on him. He concocts a "threat" to British security and seeks to inveigle Americans and others to join him. The dictator has tweaked the lion's tail. He and others like him must be taught a lesson. Besides, there is oil to consider.

The Americans are appalled. The dictator, replies the president, is no threat to world peace or to anyone but his own people. War would destabilise the region and propagate anti-Western sentiment among the Arabs. It would breach numerous treaties and be seen as imperialist. Besides, what of the United Nations? It must be given time to consider Britain's case. That is what it is for.

The British prime minister will have none of this. The UN, he says, is for wimps, a place of stallers and cowards. America should understand that the world has moved on and faces new threats. The dictator is so monstrous that treaties and laws no longer hold. America should remember Mussolini and Hitler. It should be more concerned for the security of Israel. If Washington lacks the guts for war, Britain will go it alone. The American president demurs. "From this point onwards", he says, "our views diverge."

I have immersed myself in the Suez crisis – such being the above – through reading the remarkable 1955–6 correspondence between Anthony Eden and Dwight Eisenhower [University of North Carolina Press, review in TLS]. Although fragments have been used in histories of the period, the complete letters have not appeared before. They show an astonishingly precise role reversal between Europe and America then and now.

Eisenhower emerges from the Suez letters as a counsellor of maturity and judgment, distressed to see an old friend embarking on disaster. He rebukes Eden as a latter-day imperialist, lacking a strategic vision and unable to keep global threats in proportion. He shows an America aware of the realpolitik of the Middle East, while Britain proclaims a duty to set the world to rights.

Hegel bids us learn from the mistakes of history, but offers no guidance as to which bits of history are mistakes. The parallels between Suez and Iraq are seductive. But just as Eden could mistakenly cite Hitler during Suez, so we should be wary in citing Suez in Iraq. Both were "optional" wars. The first was a disaster, destroying Eden and leaving the canal closed for 20 years. The second is still a matter of debate.

On 7 July 2005 London had a taste of what New York endured on 9/11. Bombs exploded in the Underground and on a London bus, killing 52 people. It was an unprecedented terrorist disaster. There was little panic, despite clear inadequacies in the emergency service response. London had experienced such bombs before, courtesy of the IRA. I found myself at the scene of one of them, in Euston Road.

10.07.2005

THE NATION'S response was put with dignity by Tony Blair on Thursday. He does these things well. So does London. As a city it has much in common with New York, but there is something in its genes, in the understatement of its architecture and its gentler urban language, that renders Londoners immune to panic. At Euston Road I saw rescuers, victims, passers-by, all calm, as if in dignified ritual. Normalcy defied terror. This could only be London.

The difficult part comes next. A wise general keeps sight of his enemy's objective. The terrorist's objective is not to kill but, by doing so, to publicise his cause and incite a violent and repressive response. Blair said on Thursday that "the purpose of the terrorist is to terrorise". True. But why then the stomach-churning media hyperbole that surrounds these incidents? It is one thing to report, another to wallow in grief pornography as if the bomb itself were a celebrity.

After 9/11 Britain joined America in a retaliatory attack on Afghanistan, killing far more people than had died in America. The result ever since has been an unstable Afghanistan and increased hostility to the West across the Muslim world. Blair is right to insist that bombing London serves no purpose beyond inciting anti-Muslim sentiment. But why does he not apply that logic conversely to the bombing of Iraq? We must hope and pray that Blair, with George Bush in attendance, does not use Thursday as an excuse to kick hell out of another poor country in their "War on Terror".

Thursday's bombs are crimes, a failure of domestic policing, yet one from which no city can be immune. They are not politically significant. They do not impoverish millions or alter the balance of world power. They are not an act of war between states, actual or virtual. They in no way diminish Britain's national security or way of life. We are too robust.

Throughout the age of intervention and the War on Terror, there was no rational relationship between these random atrocities – in New York, London, Bali and Madrid – and the projection of armies against states. Were the atrocities meant to be anarchist or retaliatory? Were the armies intended to be punitive or preventive? The London bombers left statements directly linking their action to the wars in Afghanistan and Iraq: "Your democratically-elected governments continuously perpetuate atrocities against my people all over the world. And your support of them makes you directly responsible." Yet politicians and the media were reluctant to accept any such link, lest it appear in Muslim eyes to justify the concept of jihad.

In reality there was a growing disjunction between the various elements in the West's interventions. What were they trying to achieve? What was the endgame in each theatre? In Iraq these questions became the more intractable over the summer of 2005 as internal security headed towards collapse. Sunni and Shi'a militias were now bombing, shooting and kidnapping across Baghdad. The civilian death rate rose to its highest since the invasion. The role of foreign troops in the country was increasingly provocative. Their presence was resented on all sides and their status was uncertain under a supposedly devolved Iraqi government. They seemed a mercenary army, largely devoted to protecting the new administration. But they still dared not leave.

21.09.2005

Don't be fooled a second time. They told you Britain must invade Iraq because of its weapons of mass destruction. They were wrong. Now they say British troops must stay in Iraq because otherwise it will collapse into chaos. This second lie is infecting everyone. It is spouted by Labour and Tory opponents of the war and even by the Liberal Democrat spokesman, Sir Menzies Campbell. Its axiom is that Western soldiers are so competent that, wherever they go, only good can result. It is their duty not to leave Iraq until order is established, infrastructure rebuilt and democracy entrenched.

Note the word "until". It hides a bloodstained half century of Western self-delusion and arrogance. The white man's burden is still alive and well in the skies over Baghdad (the streets are now too dangerous). Soldiers and civilians may die by the hundred. Money may be squandered by the millions. But Tony Blair tells us that only Western values enforced by the barrel of a gun can save the hapless Mussulman from his worst enemy, himself.

When I was in Iraq two years ago the south was, in its own terms, a success. While the Americans were unleashing mayhem to the north, the British were methodically applying Lugard-style colonialism in Basra. They formed alliances with sheikhs, bribed warlords and won hearts and minds by going about un-armoured. There was optimism in the air.

That policy demanded one thing, momentum towards local sovereignty and early withdrawal. There was no such momentum.

An ever more confident insurrection was allowed first to impede and then dictate the timetable of withdrawal. The 150,000 foreign troops on Iraqi soil are overwhelmingly committed to self-protection. They do not do law and order any more. Power is finding its new locus, in the mafias, sheikhdoms, militias and warlords that flourish amid anarchy. Where there is no security, the gunman is always king.

The alleged reason for occupying Iraq was to build security and democracy. We have dismantled the first and failed to construct the second. Iraq is a fiasco without parallel in recent British policy. Now we are told that we must "stay the course" or worse will befall. This is code for ministers refusing to admit a mistake and hoping someone else will do so after they are gone. By then the Kurds will be more detached, the Sunnis more enraged and the Shi'as more fundamentalist. A hundred British soldiers will have died.

America left Vietnam and Lebanon to their fate. They survived. We left Aden and other colonies. Some, such as Malaya and Cyprus, saw bloodshed and partition. We said rightly that this was their business. So too is Iraq for the Iraqis. We have made enough mess there already.

The coalition troops stayed, all 180,000 of them, incarcerated in the mightiest fortresses ever built by America overseas. In October a referendum approved a new constitution and in December a new assembly was put to the voters. That month I again visited Iraq, including to the British army under increasing pressure in Basra. The security situation was incomparably worse than on my previous visit. Soldiers no longer patrolled on foot in berets but in heavily armoured cars. But there had been political progress. Again the hope was that this might enable an early withdrawal. Again I was over-optimistic.

01.01.2006

THE GOOD news is that 2006 will see the effective end of the Western occupation of Iraq. It will end because everyone will be exhausted, the Americans, the British, the Iraqis and their neighbours. It will end because all justification for its continuance will have evaporated.

The election whose result is to be declared next week is good news. The federal constitution fashioned by the American ambassador, Zalmay Khalilzad, is good news. The resulting coalition government will be good news since it will put the strongest group, the cleric-backed pro-Iranian Sciri, in effective power. But all this good news will depend on one thing, the new government being seen to stand on its own feet. It must have the legitimacy and authority to forge its own alliances and hack its own deals. As long as its land is pockmarked with fortresses stuffed with 180,000 foreign troops, such independence will be unreal. Such a government will continue to be treated as an American puppet.

On 22 December Tony Blair paid his Christmas call on British troops in Basra to tell them how much things were improving. This time he said security was "completely changed" from last year. What he meant was unclear. It was as if Gladstone had visited Gordon during the siege of Khartoum and told him things were fine. Did Blair not find it strange that he could not move outside his fortress, could not drive anywhere or talk to any Iraqis? Did he wonder why British troops have withdrawn from two provinces?

Reliable reporting from Iraq is now so dangerous that the level of insecurity can be gleaned only from circumstantial evidence. Baghdad outside the American green zone is now all "red zone", off limits to any but the most reckless foreigner. The death rate and the number of explosions are rising. While some rural areas are relatively safe there is no such thing as national security. Iraq's borders are porous. Crime is uncontrolled. The concept of an "occupying power" is near meaningless.

The Americans cannot even protect the lawyers at Saddam's trial, two of whom have already been killed. Iraqis are meeting violent death in greater numbers probably than at any time since Saddam's massacre of Shi'as in 1991. Professionals are being driven into exile, children are kidnapped, women are forced indoors or shot for being improperly dressed. Those Britons who preen themselves for "bringing democracy to Iraq" would not dare visit the place.

The exit strategy at present relies on there being a fixed moment when the Iraqi army will pass some notional Sandhurst test. It will be "ready to take on the insurgents" and thus "prevent civil war". Such talk has long brought comfort to the armchairs of Pall Mall. The concept of locals being "almost ready" to replace our boys has long appealed to the imperial imagination.

I can attest to the courage of Iraq's officers and the commitment of its instructors. But I was constantly being taken aside and told that it was inconceivable that these soldiers would obey an order from a partisan minister in Baghdad to advance against distant militias, except under American protection. As for the police, basis of law and order, they are a long-lost cause.

I was told by a senior British security official last month that the Iraq experience had been so ghastly that no British government would do anything like it "for a very long time indeed". Funny, I thought. Why has it just been announced that 4,000 British troops are to leave to fight the Taliban in southern Afghanistan, whence even the Americans have fled? Nobody can give me an answer.

9

Return to Afghanistan

By the spring of 2006 it was clear that the "defeat" of the Taliban in Afghanistan had been no more complete than the suppression of the Sunni or Shi'a insurgents in Iraq. The enemy had merely retreated from the capital and regrouped, drawing popular strength from each continuing month of foreign occupation. The Taliban was proving particularly strong in the chief opium-producing province of Helmand. In 2005 this was allotted to NATO's British contingent to pacify, partly by wiping out the opium crop. There were conflicting views as to how easy this wholly fanciful exercise would prove.

04.01.2006

IN THE next few weeks, an army of 3,400 British troops expect to be deployed to Helmand province in southern Afghanistan. This is nearly half the number deployed in Iraq. Everything I have heard and read about this expedition suggests that it makes no sense. British soldiers are being sent to a poor and dangerous place whose sole economic resource is opium. They will sit there as targets for probably the most intractable coalition of insurgents, Taliban, drug traffickers and suicide bombers. They will stay until some minister has the guts to withdraw them.

Even the context of this expedition is obscure. The Afghan War was supposedly won and the Taliban defeated in 2001. It is fashionable, even in circles opposed to the Iraq War, to claim Afghanistan as a triumph. The Americans and British bombed the hell out of whatever was left of Kabul by the Russians and the invading Taliban. A ramshackle army of warlords and mercenaries was helped back into power and the status quo ante to the Taliban was restored. That would have been the best time to leave.

As it was, neo-imperialists in Washington and London couldn't resist attempting that Everest of nation-building, a new Afghanistan. Their engaging puppet, Hamid Karzai, rules an increasingly insecure landscape, wholly dependent on Western aid and a booming narco-economy. Outside Kabul, the country appears to be in the hands of a disparate federation of local rulers, tribal warlords and Taliban commanders, all afloat on a sea of opium. The drug is the basis of half Afghanistan's domestic output and virtually all its export and personal wealth.

The Americans are wisely treating this country as history. They are reducing their troops to some 10,000 at the Bagram base, dedicated to pursuing George Bush's Scarlet Pimpernel, Osama bin Laden. The rest of the country is being handed over to role-hungry NATO. But NATO has no clue what to do. The French, Germans and Spaniards want no part in the madcap venture. The Canadians and Dutch are nervous, so much so that the Dutch may pull out. That leaves the British, mostly with the turbulent province of Helmand.

The defence secretary, John Reid, said last month that the expedition's mission is to promote security, which is "absolutely interlinked to countering narcotics". This is to be achieved "by helping growers with an alternative economic livelihood". This cannot make sense. There is no way 3,000 British troops can handle the Taliban reinforced by drug profits. As for countering those profits, opium is to Helmand what oil is to Kuwait.

Eradicating Afghanistan's poppy crop was assigned to Britain after the 2001 war. Before Clare Short arrived to oversee this task, poppies were grown in just six of the 32 provinces. By the time she finished, the UN recorded production in 28 provinces and a record export value of $2.3bn. It was probably Britain's most successful agricultural policy of all time.

In Chicago in 1999, Tony Blair set out five preconditions for British military intervention in the new century. They included legal certainty, military prudence and a clear national interest at stake. None is met in Helmand. Someone should make Blair read General Sir Rupert Smith's recent study, *The Utility of Force*. His view is that an exaggerated faith in hi-tech armies against insurgency is now leading the West to create one ruined nation after another.

Smith points out that operations such as those in Somalia, Afghanistan and Iraq are not like the Falklands or Gulf wars, where the military aim was to eject an enemy army from occupied territories. They are rather "wars among the people", in which missiles, gunships, fortified bases and search-and-destroy missions are usually counterproductive. The enemy is not a state, vulnerable to "kinetic force projection". It is a miasma of conspiracies, loyalties and lasting hostilities, whose combatants know no boundaries. The influence of outside armies over the outcome of such conflict can only be informal and limited.

The Helmand expedition arises from Blair's obsession with global machismo and his addiction to abstract nouns. If I were its designated leader, General David Richards, I would grab Reid by the lapels, ram his head against the ministry wall and scream: "Tell me what the hell you really mean by sending my soldiers to that godawful place?" If the reply is yet more waffle about upholding democracy and combating terror, I would storm out with such a door slam as could be heard the length of Britain.

The Helmand expedition bore no coherent relationship to the new interventionism. It was an exercise in classic insurgency suppression reminiscent of the last days of the British Empire. Indeed, when I challenged him Richards could only reply that "it worked in Malaya". British troops now found themselves engaged in not one but two low-intensity wars. It was impossible to see the exit strategy in either case.

19.02.2006

Is Osama bin Laden winning after all? Until recently I would have derided such a thought. How could a tinpot fanatic who is either dead or shut in some mountain hideout hold the world to ransom for five years? It would stretch the imagination of an Ian Fleming.

Now I am beginning to wonder. Not a day passes without some new sign of Bin Laden's mesmeric grip on the governments of Britain and America. His deeds lie behind half the world's headlines. British policy seems obsessed with one word: terrorism. The West is equivocating, writhing, slithering in precisely the direction most desired by its enemy. He must be roaring with delight.

On any objective measure, terrorism in the West is a trivial crime. True, New York and London saw outrages in 2001 and 2005 respectively. Both were the outcome of sloppy intelligence. Neither has been repeated. Policing has improved and probably averted other attacks. Vigilance is important but only those with money in security have an interest in presenting Bin Laden as a cosmic threat.

If ever there is a case for collective restraint it is in response to terrorism. The word refers to a technique not an ideology. A bombing is an anarchic gesture calling for police and medical services. It becomes a political weapon only if publicised and answered with hysteria. A killing is so staged as to cause over-reaction, violent response, mass arrests and a decay of civilised values. Bin Laden's intention in 2001 was to portray the West as scared, emotionally vulnerable, over-reactive, decadent and careless of liberal values. The West has done its damnedest to prove him right.

There is now a voluminous literature on the politics of fear and its distorting appeal for democratic leaders [David Runciman's *The Politics of Good Intentions* and Peter Oborne's *The Use and Abuse of Terror*]. The 9/11 "changes everything" mantra began as an explanation of a national trauma. But there never was a "terrorist threat" to Western civilisation or democracy, only to Western lives and property. The threat becomes systemic only when democracy loses its confidence and when its leaders are weak, as now.

Terror attacks are for the police. For George Bush and Blair to demand a "long war" against Bin Laden and, by implication, a long suppression of civil liberty is ludicrous. Western civilisation is not some simpering weakling that cowers before a fanatic's might, pleading for leaders to protect it by all means. It has been proof against Islamic expansionism since the seventeenth century. It is not at risk.

As if on cue, a new enemy now strayed into the sights of the West. Iran's ayatollahs had long been members of George W. Bush's "axis of evil", yet they remained immune to outside pressure. Iran was just too big, with 77 million inhabitants almost three times the size of Iraq and with an entrenched military establishment. Now reports of Iran developing a nuclear capability thrust it into Tony Blair's chamber of imagined horrors. Here at last might be some real weapons of mass destruction claiming his interventionist zeal.

12.04.2006

THIS WEEK'S most terrifying remark came from the foreign secretary, Jack Straw. He declared that a nuclear attack on Iran would be "completely nuts" and an assault of any sort "inconceivable". In Straw-speak, "nuts" can mean he's just heard it might happen and "inconceivable" can mean certain.

A measure of the plight of British foreign policy is that such words from the foreign secretary are anything but reassuring. Straw says of Iran that "there is no smoking gun, there is no *casus belli*". There was no smoking gun in Iraq, only weapons conjured from the fevered imagination of Downing Street and its intelligence chiefs. It is a racing certainty that Alastair Campbell look-alikes are even now cajoling MI6's John Scarlett into proving that Iran is "far closer" to a bomb than anyone thinks.

As for a *casus belli*, there was none in Iraq. Tony Blair had to beat one out of his hapless attorney general before his generals would agree to fight. Iran's *casus belli* was set out in unambiguous terms by the prime minister in his speech to the Foreign Policy Centre in London on 21 March. Blair was updating his 1999 Chicago doctrine of global intervention. Then it was justified by humanitarianism and was optional. Now it is vital for the "battle of values ... a battle about modernity". Those who are not of our values are to be subject to pre-emptive attack.

Blair demanded that the West become "active not reactive" against alien values (obviously Islamic) as "we risk chaos threatening our stability". The crusade against them was "utterly determinative of our future here in Britain". He accepted that Britain should seek international agreement before going to war, but should still fight without it. People were crying out for democracy. We must bring it to them since "in their salvation lies our own security".

The speech was full of jihadist rhetoric. Blair's desire to wipe non-democratic values off the map is akin to Iran's view of Israel. But we know that when he says war he means war. The speech was the wildest by a British leader in modern times. Blair mentioned Iran three times. It was gilt-edged, copper-bottomed, swivel-eyed neo-conservatism.

To such a world view, Iran is a far more magnetic target than Iraq. Elements within its regime want nuclear weapons. The country is rich and capable of buying the relevant components. The mullahs have sponsored terrorist groups abroad and fiddled elections. In February, President Mahmoud Ahmadinejad restarted uranium enrichment at the Natanz plant, in defiance of the UN, and yesterday Iran's nuclear energy chief announced that it had proved successful. What does Straw mean, "no *casus belli*"?

Confrontation without a willingness to use total force is bluff. Many Iranian hardliners must be itching to cause more trouble in Iraq, threaten tanker lanes in the Straits of Hormuz and set Asian opinion further against the West. This is one country in the region that has retained some political pluralism. It has shown bursts of democratic activity and, importantly, has experienced internal regime change.

If ever there was a nation not to drive to the extreme it is Iran. If ever there was a powerful state to reassure and befriend rather than abuse and threaten, it is Iran. If ever there was a regime not to goad into seeking nuclear weapons it is Iran. Yet that is precisely what British and American policy is doing.

Meanwhile Blair had more pressing business to hand. In June of 2006 I travelled to Kabul to interview the British commander of the international security force, General David Richards. He was finally dispatching the British contingent of 3–4,000 troops to Helmand to suppress a renascent Taliban insurgency. He was in a remarkably up-beat mood and rather disappointed when I said that I would regard our conversation as off the record. He conveyed a cocky over-confidence that I found ominous. Was he aware he was going to fight the Pashtu, proud warriors down the ages with a love of fighting and a celebrated ability to bear a grudge?

07.06.2006

RICHARDS IS running a sort of peace-keeping Olympics, with soldiers from 36 nations – from Luxembourg to Mongolia – all out to prove their new-world-order spurs. He must somehow do what has defied the Americans for four years: curb the resurgent Taliban, impose government on the provinces and persuade local rulers to pay allegiance and taxes to Kabul. This would be for the first time in their history.

Down south the Americans have failed to stem increasing Taliban infiltration from Pakistan. Their brutal bombing of villages has recruited hundreds of fighters to the Taliban cause and bred hatred for the Americans and for Karzai. On Thursday the Taliban almost killed the Canadian commander in Kandahar.

Richards must try to reverse of all this. He is certainly the kind of soldier I would put in any ditch. He would defend Rourke's Drift to the final bullet and pin down an entire Panzer brigade to cover the Dunkirk retreat. His strategy is to draw a thick line under the heavy-handed American tactics and go for hearts and minds in selected "ink spots".

The trouble is Richards has no control over the Americans, obsessed with tracking down the Scarlet Pimpernel, Osama bin Laden, by hook or crook, mostly crook. The original American policy had realpolitik. It was to capture Kabul with proxy tribesmen, topple the regime and get out fast. Even the most starry-eyed neo-con could see little thanks in nation-building in Kabul. But the policy needed cover for its retreat. It needed a fall guy.

Step forward plucky Britain, with Afghan glory lodged in its military genes. This time it even came with a glittering baggage train of cosmopolitan hangers-on. The fall guy will fall but we can take comfort that he will do it in style.

The age of intervention took me to strange places, but few stranger than Kabul. By 2006 – after five years of interventionist war – it was the citadel of a nation under siege. There were shanty towns of tribes driven from their land, merchants hawking their wares and the dust clouds of the white 4-by-4s of NGO aristocrats. Rumours were of provinces falling and main roads impassable. The cities of Kandahar and Talalabad were reachable only by military helicopter. Kabul's once-delightful streets bore the scars of decades of civil war.

09.06.2006

Until the 1970s Kabul was an ethereal place of baked mud houses and gardens nestling among the foothills of the Hindu Kush. It was "the light garden of the angel king". It then spent a quarter-century being bombed and shelled by Russians, the Taliban, Afghan tribes and Western jets. Eventually most of it just sighed and sank to its knees in despair, its heart reduced to acres of dust-blown filth. Fragments of crumbling walls still loom from the ruins, like pictures of Dresden after the war. Inhabitants crawl into basement hovels or squat on the bed of the once-blue Kabul river, now a trickle of sewage.

My guidebook remarks that the best advice for a visitor to Afghanistan is "to get out of the capital as soon as you can". Any charms are on the outskirts: the restored burial garden of Babur, the first Mughal emperor; the royal mausoleum; the ruins of the great fortress of Bala Hissar; the old Timurid pottery village of Istalif, now reviving after being flattened by Taliban shells.

Nobody mentions the old city in central Kabul. Yet historic quarters form the emotional focus of all great cities. That is why they are treasured in places as diverse as Warsaw, Barcelona, Cairo and Delhi. In such quarters citizens find their identity and visitors glimpse the uniqueness of a country and its culture. Enough remains of old Kabul to be worth repairing or reconstructing. It requires only an effort of will and persuasion.

Does anyone care? Modern Kabul is in thrall to tens of thousands of frightened UN officials, NGO expatriates and foreign soldiers, few of whom stray from their compounds, either into the old city or out into the wild surrounding country. Some do good work in medicine and education, but most commune with each other in heavily guarded villas and armoured Land Cruisers. The NGO "swarm" is now the cultural aftershock of modern war. I am told the going rate to run Britain's one-day "gender awareness" course for Afghan women is £40,000, including T-shirts.

The West is spending obscene amounts on the military occupation of Afghanistan, including a £1bn base in Helmand. Spending is no less obscene on trying (and failing) to suppress the country's only export crop, opium, which Britain consumes in vast quantities. For a fraction of this money, Kabul could have restored to it some of the dignity it has lost over the past quarter-century. For a smaller fraction, London could at least restore the magnificent old British legation. It stands rotting and derelict in its park while diplomats cower in buildings rented from Bulgarians.

Curzon's greatest legacy to India was not pomp or civil service. It was saving the Taj Mahal, Fatehpur Sikri and a hundred palaces, castles and temples that are India's glory and its most precious tourist asset. Nehru later said of Curzon that he would be remembered most among viceroys because he saved "all that is beautiful in India". It was Curzon's proudest boast. Will the same be said of his successors on this side of the North-West Frontier?

All advice from intelligence sources in Kabul ran flatly counter to what was being heard, or at least said, in London. This Afghanistan mismatch of optimism at headquarters and pessimism at the front was a classic syndrome of armies engaged in foreign wars. Yet no one seemed aware of this. Hundreds of British soldiers were about to be sent to their possible deaths in Helmand on the basis of what were blatantly false expectations. It was astonishingly incompetent.

05.07.2006

The House of Commons should begin its post-mortem now. The questions for it to answer are legion. What had Kabul ever had to do with NATO? Who created the peace-keeping convention of 36 nation's armies now in Kabul, many of them not members of NATO and with no intention of actually fighting? Did the defence secretary Geoff Hoon commit British troops to the hostile south – the most dangerous posting in Afghanistan – in return for gaining the first rota of NATO command?

Then again did Hoon's successor, John Reid, really believe that in mid-2005 the Taliban were just "remnants" and a "dwindling force"? This was when British officers on the ground were warning him that the south was "not Land Rover but Warrior country ... tin hats, rifles and body armour". The American 503rd infantry were suffering

10 killed and dozens wounded each month. Yet Reid declared that Britain could achieve success "without a shot fired".

Every assessment I have heard suggests that the sort of campaign envisaged by the government in Helmand would require not 3,000 or even 10,000 troops, but over 100,000. Even the latter total has failed in Iraq, and Iraqis cannot hold a candle to Afghans for insurgent fanaticism. As for opium, if the West wants poor people to grow food instead of poppies, why does it refuse to curb its heroin consumption while dumping grain surpluses on the Afghan market?

British policy in Afghanistan is so contradictory and stupid as to be beyond belief. Yet intelligent diplomats, NGOs and soldiers must spout it because that is what ministers require. Those ministers should not be let off the hook.

Last week a company of the 3rd Battalion, the Parachute Regiment, visited the Helmand village of Zumbelay in an early run of "hearts and minds". The result was vividly described by Christina Lamb of the *Sunday Times*. Tailed by spies and arriving publicly in soft hats without air cover, the soldiers tried to bribe village elders with projects to reject the Taliban. They had walked into a trap. In the resulting fire-fight they were lucky to escape a massacre.

After some ten years of military intervention and five armed conflicts, historians were seeking to set the period in some historical and ideological context. With the end of Empire and the dismantling of the Cold War's spheres of influence, most modern nations sought influence over others through subtler means than war. Free states would guide each other by example, deploy "soft power" and, where necessary, pursue "intervention-lite". They traded, taught each other's young, took in each other's refugees. But they were careful to tolerate each other's religions and, above all, respect each other's territory. All these maxims seemed at risk in the age of intervention.

13.08.2006

HARVARD'S JOSEPH Nye described America's imperial power as "velvet hegemony". With exceptions it has remained the "shining city upon the hill", its power lying in the magnetism of example.

"A country may obtain the outcomes it wants in world politics", wrote Nye, "because other countries want to follow it ... admiring its values and aspiring to its level of prosperity and openness."

Every American action in the Middle East these past five years has polluted these words. The wreckage of security, the lack of order, the abuse of international law, the corruption of aid and atrocities on land, from the air and in prisons. All have rotted the moral supremacy that alone can legitimise intervention in a foreign state.

Most unexpected has been the sheer incompetence of these interventions. There are now some 50 books on 9/11 and its aftermath. Each is a tale of ineptitude. The hijacking of the West's military industrial complex by an inexperienced cabal of neoconservatives must rank among the great follies of modern history.

Lawrence Wright's *The Looming Tower* and Thomas Ricks's *Fiasco*, catalogue brave men fighting against the odds (usually their own side). But overall they offer a litany of warnings neglected, intelligence abused, feuding generals, stupefying waste and a general disregard for victims of the technology of war. Every Pentagon tactic seems to have played into the hands of militant Islam. It has been a rerun of the fourth crusade.

As the Israelis are finding in southern Lebanon (and the US marines in Falluja and the British in Helmand), high-tech war has no response to faith in a cause or desire for revenge at the violation of one's country. Big is blundering. The mice have roared at Western power projection. Bush and Blair have needlessly alienated a continent and put their peoples at risk of terrorist retaliation. Now they need a plan B and fast, a plan for global humility. They need to return to imperialism soft. They should shine their city on the hill and stop killing people on the plain.

Above all, intervention needed some ethical coherence it should meet Kant's moral imperative, that it be universal in its application or it loses force, both as a moral rule and as a deterrent. Otherwise it will collapse into opportunism and hypocrisy.

In the autumn of 2006 the horror of civil war in Sudan's Darfur was coming increasingly to world attention. Tens of thousands were now

dying from sectarian conflict in the desert. As always the cry went up that "something must be done". But what policy might guide military as opposed to charitable intervention in such desperate places? Why was the West prepared to expend lives and treasure on the ailments of Asia but not on Africa?

20.09.2006

MACHISMO IN foreign policy always has the best tunes, but tunes are not enough. They are highly selective, relating chiefly to television coverage. The reluctance of interveners (mostly Britain and America) to come to the aid of Tibetans, Chechens, Zimbabweans or Kashmiris may be realpolitik. But the neglect of Congolese, Sri Lankans, Burmese or Uzbeks – with political and humanitarian outrages aplenty – is odd. If Sierra Leone, why not Somalia? If East Timor, why not Aceh? Why are we so tolerant of that nuclear host to terror, dictatorial Pakistan, yet so hysterical towards semi-democratic Iran? And what of Sudan?

Nothing has changed since Kipling asked: "When you've shouted Rule Britannia / When you've sung God Save the Queen / When you've finished killing Kruger with your mouth … " what then? The swelling chorus of something-must-be-done-in-Darfur argues that such talk at least "raises awareness". They ask, what would you do about the [Sudanese government's militia] the Janjaweed, and what about the 1.9 million refugees?

My answer is in substance identical to theirs: nothing really. The Janjaweed are not in my country, are not my business and, most important, are not a problem within my power to solve. The difficulty is that international politics has yet to find a way of expressing these distinctions. The UN may no longer adhere to non-intervention in member states' internal affairs, but it has no ideology of proportionate aggression to replace it. This leaves the field open to "jihadists" on all sides.

As it is, spasmodic and selective damnation of distant states shows the West as a paper tiger. It incites rebels and separatists to anticipate Western support, which is why such support almost always leads to partition, Yugoslavia and Iraq being the most recent examples. As for the "coward's war" of sanctions, they only entrench regimes, hurt the poor and drive the middle class and opposition into exile.

Today's constant banging of the aggressor's drum makes embattled regimes resist the one intervention that is usually most urgent: humanitarian relief. Helping the starving and dying, monitoring their fate and protecting their relief should be the first responsibility of the international community. In Africa and elsewhere the involvement of charities in conflicts has become controversial. All relief is aid, and all aid is in some sense political. The more reason to uphold the purity of vision of the Red Cross pioneers, to help the needy without taking sides.

10

Endgame Eludes Iraq, Again

My forecasts of endgame in Iraq were becoming tedious. Few could have believed that Western troops would still be occupying the country four years after the invasion. It was clear that George W. Bush too could hardly believe it. Yet the failure of the new Iraqi government to impose order and a rising tide of Sunni/Shiʻa violence were rendering the country as unstable as ever. All talk was of a Western withdrawal – and of its impossibility. The American general David Petraeus duly proposed a final "surge", one last push for victory.

07.01.2007

THIS IS the week, we are told, when George Bush will announce positively the last military assault on insurgency in Iraq before he finally loses patience and quits. The so-called surge will supposedly correct the mistake of last year's Operation Together Forward. Without order in the capital the physical and political reconstruction of Iraq is impossible. But since that order cannot, after all, be assigned to Iraqi forces, the Americans must throw another 20,000–30,000 troops into the conflict.

I have not heard one plausible game plan for the "Battle of the Surge". Leaks have indicated that commanders on the ground are strongly opposed to giving the enemy yet more targets. Pentagon chiefs are equally opposed to the cost in men and money of a transient boost in control on the ground. American public opinion and Congress are overwhelmingly against the plan, which Chuck Hagel, the Republican senator, calls "Alice in Wonderland".

Leaders contemplating defeat far from the front are always tempted to order "one last push". Thus did Hitler order the Battle of the Bulge, Nixon the bombing of Cambodia and Reagan the blasting of the Shouf to cover his retreat from Beirut. A general must pretend to victory even in the jaws of defeat, or his soldiers will not fight. America has one million men under arms. Surely they are not to be beaten by a few hundred guerrillas in the suburbs of Baghdad? So Bush will tell them to make one last heave, however pointless. He does not want to share his father's legacy of cutting and running from Iraq.

Such Iraqi government as exists under Nouri al-Maliki, the prime minister, is unable to enforce any law or command any army. For Washington and London to tell him to "bring his militias to heel" is like telling a junior cop to arrest Al Capone. Large areas of Iraq are under the rough and ready control of either clerical fundamentalists or gangsters rich on stolen American aid. Baghdad is given over to lethal roadblocks, nocturnal disappearances and mass killings. A million Iraqis have left the country since the Americans arrived, including an estimated 40 per cent of the professional class. Only the green zone operates as a working entity and its isolation is medieval, its inhabitants barely able to venture beyond its walls.

As the Iraq surge unfolded, the increased danger faced by troops on the ground meant that more infantry operations called in air support. By its nature this was inaccurate and reliant on notoriously unreliable local intelligence. The leaking of a film of one such "friendly fire" incident and its dissemination via social media caused widespread anger.

07.02.2007

WATCHING A person kill another is the purest horror. Watching it done from the air, from a sanitised distance, is somehow less so. Distance launders the bloodletting and technology purifies it. War becomes another video game. The camera sees no broken bodies. If it sees a mistake it does not see the mistake that caused the mistake.

The video-recording of the attack by two American jets on a British column in Iraq in March 2003, which caused the death of Corporal Matty Hull, should be in any museum of war. We hear the pilots clearly hungry for targets and finding them. They question the identity of the column, which seems to have "friendly" markings, but ground control assures them it is not friendly. They attack, and they crow as they score. Ground control calmly tells them they have made a mistake and to head for home. They curse, weep and cry: "We're in jail ... I'm going to be sick." They have killed their own.

When bombing from the air kills non-combatants, as it does to an appalling degree, there should at least be a military inquiry into why. This, if nothing else, vindicates the publicity given to the Hull case. Massacres committed by infantrymen are subject to courts martial. If soldiers enter a house by the front door and kill civilians inside, they are hauled before world opinion and condemned. If a dropped bomb enters the same house through the roof and has the same effect, it is dismissed as collateral damage. In Iraq it is not even recorded.

That military strategy is so casual about bomb inaccuracy is largely due to the technological glamour attached to air forces as against ground troops. The latter are always worse equipped and worse protected. Air commanders have long oversold the efficacy of strategic bombing and ignore the degree to which, in counter-insurgency war, such bombardment can be counter-productive. The destruction of non-military targets and the incidental killing of civilians is far more damaging to the cause of victory than friendly-fire casualties that attract so much publicity and inquiry.

The recent recourse of British troops in Afghanistan to aerial bombardment has, by general agreement, set back the cause of winning hearts and minds. Britain is now fighting two wars which it is losing. In such circumstances the killing of the enemy appears to be the only policy that delivers good news. In Iraq and Afghanistan kill rates have taken on the symbolic role they served in Vietnam. "We may not be winning but they are hurting", is the general's desperate cry. Yesterday we were shown how good bombers are at hurting, but how bad they are at winning. They are war at its most stupid.

On my visits to Iraq I sought out the surviving monuments of one of the world's most ancient civilisations. It was a depressing and increasingly dangerous thing to do. The state of the country made a mockery of the word civilisation.

There were few more lasting memorials to the US–British occupation of Iraq than the destruction and dispersal of that country's antiquities. Ancient Mesopotamian sites were left unguarded and looted. Baghdad's great museum, trashed at the time of the invasion, was supposedly restored but never reopened to the public. Fewer than half the estimated 15,000 objects stolen after the invasion were returned. A nation's present can be recreated, but never its past. Was this the most lasting legacy of intervention?

08.06.2007

FLY INTO the American air base of Tallil outside Nasiriya in central Iraq and the flight path is over the great ziggurat of Ur, reputedly the earliest city on earth. Seen from the base in the desert haze or the sand-filled gloom of dusk, the structure is indistinguishable from fuel dumps, stores and hangars. Ur is safe within a compound. But its walls are pockmarked with wartime shrapnel and a blockhouse is being built over an adjacent archaeological site. When the head of Iraq's supposedly sovereign board of antiquities and heritage, Abbas al-Hussaini, tried to inspect the site recently, the Americans refused him access to his own most treasured monument.

Yesterday Hussaini reported to the British Museum on his struggles to protect his works in a state of anarchy. It was a heart-breaking presentation. Under Saddam you were likely to be tortured and shot if you let someone steal an antiquity; in today's Iraq you are likely to be tortured and shot if you don't. The tragic fate of the national museum in Baghdad in April 2003 was as if federal troops had invaded New York city, sacked the police and told the criminal community that the Metropolitan was at their disposal. The local tank commander was told specifically not to protect the museum for a full two weeks after the invasion. Even the Nazis protected the Louvre.

When I visited the museum six months later, its then director, Donny George, proudly showed me the best he was making of a bad job. He was about to reopen, albeit with half his most important objects stolen. The pro-war lobby had stopped pretending that the looting was nothing to do with the Americans, who were shamefacedly helping retrieve stolen objects under a dynamic colonel,

Michael Bogdanos (author of a recent book on the subject). The vigorous Italian "cultural envoy to the coalition", Mario Bondioli-Osio, was giving generously for restoration.

The beautiful Warka vase, carved in 3000 BC, was recovered though smashed into 14 pieces. The exquisite Lyre of Ur, the world's most ancient musical instrument, was found badly damaged. Clerics in Sadr City were ingeniously asked to tell wives to refuse to sleep with their husbands if looted objects were not returned, with some success. Nothing could be done about the national library gutted by American bombs, and the loss of five centuries of Ottoman records (and works by Piccasso and Miro).

Today the picture is transformed. Donny George fled for his life last August after death threats. The national museum is not open but shut. Nor is it just shut. Its doors are actually bricked up and the building surrounded by concrete walls. The exhibits are sandbagged. Even the staff cannot get inside. There is no prospect of reopening.

As long as Britain and America remain in denial over the anarchy they have created in Iraq, they clearly feel they must deny its devastating side-effects. Two million refugees camping in Jordan and Syria are ignored, since life in Iraq is supposed to be "better than before". Likewise dozens of Iraqis working for the British and thus facing death threats are denied asylum. To grant it would mean the former defence and now home secretary, John Reid, admitting his promise of security was wrong. They will die before he does that.

That Western civilisation should have been born in so benighted a country as Iraq may seem bad luck. But only now is that birth being refused all guardianship, in defiance of international law. If this is Tony Blair's "values war", then language has lost all meaning.

On 27 June 2007 Tony Blair resigned as prime minister. Two months later, at dead of night on 3 September, British troops withdraw from their Basra base, having failed to establish stable government in the province. They now hunkered down in the airport compound. The retreat was widely seen as a British defeat, at a time when the American "surge" in Baghdad was being presented as a success. I was not sure this criticism was fair.

09.09.2007

THE AMERICAN and British armies do not have to withdraw from Iraq. They are powerful and can stay as long as they wish. Their governments are a different matter. They need reasons for occupying foreign countries and now face humiliation in the greatest war of ideological intervention since Vietnam. They are praying for their armies to save them from this humiliation.

This week David Petraeus, the talented American general in Baghdad, reports on the progress of his "surge" strategy to an impatient Congress. Two thirds of Americans have joined two thirds of world opinion in wanting a swift American withdrawal, defined as inside a year. Petraeus's predicament is therefore agonising. He cannot possibly offer victory. The one thing Petraeus can offer Washington is a smokescreen of partial success behind which to begin a rolling disengagement. This means a steady withdrawal of units to bases, transferring control in each enclave to whichever militia group enjoys local loyalty.

For all the abuse thrown by Americans at the British retreat in Basra, it offers a test of such withdrawal. Blood has undoubtedly flowed. Two newly autonomous provincial governors have been murdered. The Iran-backed Badr brigade has fought the local Mahdists over the spoils of victory. Deals have been cut with the Iraqi army and the militia-dominated police. The result is hardly democracy, but full-scale civil war has not broken out and living conditions appear no worse than when Britain was supposedly in charge.

Now that the chief targets of insurgency machismo, British soldiers, have departed there is a chance of a political equilibrium that might enable the people of Basra to rebuild their lives and accept aid for their battered infrastructure. That I suppose is progress.

11

Intervention Goes Viral: Tehran, Kabul, Baghdad, Rangoon, Harare

At the start of 2008 the Western world was on the brink of its worst financial collapse since the Great Depression. The collapse was brought on in part by the crippling expense of the wars of intervention. Yet for all the growing public scepticism towards those wars, the desire to intervene overseas by governments in London and Washington remained undiminished. George Bush's 9/11 motto that "he who is not with us is against us" continued to project a catch-all belligerence towards the "outside" world. It had become the foreign policy default mode.

Bush was particularly obsessed with Iran's president Mahmoud Ahmadinejad. Elected in 2005, the populist Iranian leader was facing opposition for economic policies that were causing widespread shortages and hardship. The country's capital, Tehran, was running short of petrol. Bush seemed unaware that American hostility was the one thing that bolstered Ahmadinejad's shaky regime. His hostility continued to play into the Iranian's hands.

16.01.2008

ONLY ONE man can rescue the embattled Iranian president from his growing domestic unpopularity. That man is George Bush. Ahmadinejad faces new elections in March and an increasingly disaffected clergy, but he feeds on Bush's antagonism. This week the latter duly obliged. He raced round the Middle East drumming up support for his Iranian foe.

Bush has denounced Ahmadinejad at every turn. He has offered to sanction him, embargo him, isolate him, even bomb him. He has portrayed him as a monster of evil and "leading sponsor of terror". He has showered the Saudis and the Gulf states with $20bn of weapons to confront him "before it is too late". When Ahmadinejad thanked "divine intervention" for making him president in 2005, he should also have thanked God for having first selected Bush. To have Washington as your enemy in these parts is to have everyman your friend.

In Pakistan, Bush continues to back dictatorship and must suffer the resulting Taliban "blowback" in Afghanistan. In Palestine he ignores the winner of an election, Hamas. He appeases Hosni Mubarak's dictatorship in Egypt and is craven to the autocrats of Saudi Arabia. His spokesman, Steve Hadley, challenged on what such rulers contribute to democracy, could only bumble that "these folks are on board with the freedom agenda, and are pursuing it in their own fashion". Stability trumps democracy after all.

In so far as any strategy lay behind the Bush trip, it was a hope that the monarchs of the Gulf might support the US in military action against Iran. Yet if there is one lesson these rulers know, it is to live at peace with the wilder regimes to their north. Indeed, keeping them wild suits the Gulf fine. Dubai is built on the funk money of the region. The last thing it wants is to aid America to another war, least of all with Iran.

Yet Bush does everything to generate the paranoia on which Ahmadinejad bases his electoral appeal. He threatens him with the constraint of an American war, and thus dilutes the constraint of Iranian democracy. Does Bush not realise how the threat of external attack helps an embattled leader? Has he forgotten 9/11?

Across the Iranian border in Afghanistan it was already clear that British military operations in Helmand were not proving as easy as General Richards had planned. In particular the Taliban, who after 9/11 had been increasingly hostile to the presence of al-Qaeda in their territory, was now in league with them. It was to prove a lethal and lasting alliance of convenience.

Attacks from both the Americans and the Pakistan government were rousing insurgency across Pashtunistan, from the Khyber Pass in the north to Waziristan in the south. To incur the antagonism of the Pashtu, once the Pathans, was an error embedded in the military lore of the British Empire. Fighting the Pathans was Britain's equivalent of Napoleon marching on Moscow. It was scarcely to be believed that a British army had gone half way round the world to repeat it. Was liberal interventionism reduced to this?

03.02.2008

THE AMERICAN secretary of state, Condoleezza Rice, flies to Britain this week to meet a crisis entirely of Washington's and London's creation. They have no strategy for the continuing occupation of Afghanistan. They are hanging on for dear life and praying for something to turn up. Britain in Helmand is repeating the experience of Khartoum, the Dardanelles, Singapore and Crete, of politicians who no longer read history and expect others to die for their dreams of glory.

Last week America's Afghanistan Study Group, led by generals and diplomats of impeccable credentials, reported on "a weakening international resolve and a growing lack of confidence". An Atlantic Council report was more curt: "Make no mistake, NATO is not winning in Afghanistan." The country was in imminent danger of becoming a failed state.

A clearly exasperated Robert Gates, the American defence secretary, has broken ranks with the official optimism and committed an extra 3,000 marines to the field, while sending an "unusually stern" note to Germany demanding that its 3,200 troops "meet enemy fire". Germany, like France, has rejected that plea. Yet it is urgent since the Canadians have threatened to withdraw from the south if not relieved. An equally desperate Britain is proposing to send half-trained territorials to the Helmand front, after its commanders ignored every warning that the Taliban were the toughest fighters on earth.

George W. Bush's reckless elevation of al-Qaeda after 2001 promoted a small group of alien Arab guests into global warriors for Islam. Worse, it destroyed Islamabad's hold over the Taliban. America bribed the Pakistan president Pervez Musharraf with $1 billion a year to declare a U-turn and fight his former Taliban allies. Musharraf duly broke his non-intervention treaty with the Pashtun and sent his army against them. The Taliban's influence now increases with every attack and with every American bombing of Pashtun villages.

Wise heads in Islamabad know that they must withdraw from this conflict and restore respect for tribal autonomy. There is no sensible alternative to ending military operations against the Pashtun. Like Iraq's Kurdistan, Pashtunistan is a country without a state. It has been cursed by history, but it returns that curse with interest when attacked. Fate has now handed it a starring role in Britain's nastiest war in decades, and offered it the power to wreck an emergent democracy of vital interest to the West.

To have set one of the world's most ancient and ferocious people on the warpath against both Kabul and Islamabad takes some doing. Western policy has done it.

The new British prime minister, Gordon Brown, had none of Tony Blair's love of the world stage. But he had inherited Blair's poisoned chalice. He appointed as foreign secretary the loyal Blairite, David Miliband, who in February 2008 decided to reclothe his former master's "doctrine of international community" in new and more spacious language.

At its most optimistic, intervention had brought peace of a sort to little Bosnia and Kosovo, statelets smaller than Wales. It had reverted Sierra Leone to the status of a protectorate. But the war in Afghanistan had now been underway for seven years and in Iraq for five. Neither was getting anywhere. Much of the Muslim world had been turned from friend to sullen foe. This might be thought a good moment for a British foreign secretary to pause and reflect on the state of play with liberal interventionism, perhaps with some humility. He did not do so.

13.02.2008

DAVID MILIBAND loves democracy. We all love democracy. We also love capitalism, social welfare, child health, book learning and leatherback turtles. We would like the whole world to love them too, and we stand ready to persuade it so. But do we shoot anyone who refuses? It is hardly credible that two centuries since Immanuel Kant wrestled with this oldest of ethical conundrums, a British government still cannot tell the difference between espousing a moral imperative and enforcing one.

Yesterday in Oxford the foreign secretary decided to update the 1999 Chicago speech of his then mentor, Tony Blair, in which Blair proposed a doctrine of international community. This required Britain to attack sovereign states unprovoked if this would end a violation of human rights. Blair qualified his zeal with reference to military feasibility a "readiness for long-term commitment" and "our national interest truly engaged". Like any ruler interfering in the lives of others, the motives were soon mixed and the language confused. How feasible is feasible? How long is long-term? What is an "engaged" national interest: a moral crusade or an arms deal?

Miliband brushed aside the blundering into Iraq and Afghanistan as errors of implementation rather than principle. He takes the Blair doctrine into new territory. He wants his pan-democratic world to be achieved by peaceful means, by trade, multilateral action and – his new soundbite – a "civilian surge". Should soft power fail, Miliband wants to use sanctions and send in troops, for instance through offering security guarantees to regimes that "abide by democratic rules".

Miliband calls scepticism "a retreat into a world of realpolitik". Such point scoring may do for an Oxford debate but not for bereaved army mothers now taking him to the high court, or the thousands of victims of his doctrine who see hard-power interventionism as a menace to life and order. The professor of political science at Baghdad University said yesterday that the imprisonments under Saddam were more tolerable than the weekly murders, kidnappings, militia censorship and female repression his department is suffering. Is Miliband saying, from the comfort of his office, that this man is deluded?

There is one simple way of honouring Britain's pride in its chosen system: prove it works at home better than any other. That means working tirelessly to refresh it. This is not easy, as Miliband should know in his failed bid to regenerate civic democracy. It may seem small beer, but how can he preach reform to others when he cannot achieve the tiniest reform himself?

The West can invite the world to witness the virtues of democracy. It can deploy the soft power of education, exchange, publicity and aid. But a true democrat cannot abandon Voltaire's respect for the autonomy of disagreement, let alone seek to crush it. Britain can shine its beacon abroad but it cannot impose its values on the world. It has tried too often, and has failed. This is not isolationism. It is fact.

Meanwhile Miliband's enhanced status for liberal intervention was being tested daily on the streets of Baghdad. The fifth anniversary of the occupation of Iraq passed with no sign of a withdrawal of Western troops. Indeed 2007's temporary "surge" to cover an American retreat was starting to look permanent. There was still no clear statement of objectives, no strategy for withdrawal, no reason for what was now a half-decade-long occupation of a country which, it was now accepted, had posed no threat to any Western nation. This prompted thoughts of how unclear was the boundary between occupation and "imperialism-lite".

16.03.2008

THE JOINT American–British occupation of Iraq shows no sign of ending. There has been a fall in civilian deaths due to the intensive American policing of Baghdad, legitimising and paying some 60,000 Sunni militia to fight al-Qaeda, but this is an entry rather than an exit tactic. It makes departing more rather than less hazardous. Nowhere in non-Kurdish Iraq is there a stable political or security régime. There are even indications that the anarchy of Baghdad has shifted north, witness the killing of a Christian bishop in Mosul. The relationship between Kurds and Arabs, for instance over oil and the status of Kirkuk, is dangerously unresolved.

There are two stark indicators of the state of this occupation. One is that after five years power supplies in oil-rich Iraq are still no better than they were under Saddam Hussein and many utilities are worse. The other is that no leader of the two occupying countries dares to appear in streets that he claims to have liberated.

To British participants such as Hilary Synnott, the former British administrator in Basra, most tragic was the inability to build civil order on military victory. His memoir, *Bad Days in Basra*, charts the collapse of liaison between London and Washington as the coalition lost control in autumn 2003. It was a shambles reminiscent of nineteenth-century wars. Synnott pleads for a corps of administrators not obsessed with "Whitehall's fixation with a duty of care which prevents them being exposed to the risks which soldiers face every day".

In other words, Synnott is saying that occupation-lite must mutate into imperialism-lite if such adventures are to have any hope of success. As Colin Powell warned Bush before the invasion, "You know that you're going to be owning this place." Blair's interventionism displayed that most dangerous of military illusions: that establishing a bridgehead wins a war.

British soldiers now hunkered down in Sierra Leone, Kosovo, Afghanistan and Iraq went with the noble aim of righting a wrong. But they have induced in London a renaissance of the imperial urge, the desire to impose one's own values on foreign peoples through the barrel of a gun. They do not know how to leave.

The strength of the British Empire was that both occupier and occupied expected the British to stay. Promising to leave "when the job is done" may satisfy a domestic audience but it ensures the worst of both worlds. It stirs political and financial dependency for the present while creating uncertainty about the future. The job is never done. Autonomy is not imposed but postponed. Today's imperialism-lite, by constantly debating its departure, induces instability, encourages rebellion and so undermines its declared mission.

In May 2008 a disastrous cyclone tore through Burma's Irrawaddy delta causing appalling death and destruction. The country's closed military dictatorship declined all offers of outside help, including from a naval and air relief task force that happened to be on manoeuvres in neighbouring Thailand. This force immediately headed for the scene.

Burma seemed to me the nearest to a cast-iron case for humanitarian intervention I had seen, stronger even than neglected Sudan.

It met all the conditions set out by Blair in 1999, with the incidental gain of possibly toppling one of Asia's most repressive regimes. It was something that really could be done. Yet nothing happened. The interventionists were wholly silent. I was puzzled.

11.05.2008

WHAT ARE we waiting for? Where now is liberal interventionism? More than 100,000 people are dead after a cyclone in the Irrawaddy delta, and the United Nations has declared that up to two million people, deprived of aid for a week, are at risk of death. Barely 10 per cent are reported to have received any help. The world stands ready to save them. The warehouses of Asia are crammed with supplies. Ships and planes are on standby.

Anyone who has visited this exquisite part of the world will know how resourceful, peaceable and resilient are the delta people. Like those of low-lying Bangladesh next door, they are used to extreme weather. Their agriculture is fertile and they are self-sufficient in most things. But no one can survive instant starvation and disease.

There are three giant C-130s loaded and ready in Thailand. There are American and French ships in the area, fortuitously on a disaster relief exercise, with shelters, clothing, latrines, medicines and water decontamination equipment. Above all there are helicopters, vital in an area where roads are impassable by flooding and fallen trees.

Yet the British aid minister, Douglas Alexander, said last week intervention would be "incendiary". He did not explain why even so minor an intervention as a "dump-and-run" of emergency supplies into the delta would be incendiary – compared, for instance, with his antics in Afghanistan. He cannot hold that Burma is not ripe for "liberal intervention" because the loss of life is through natural disaster rather than political or military oppression. What is this fine distinction between a massacre and what the military are now inflicting on the Burmese people? A corpse is a corpse.

This catastrophe is not past but continuing. A Western world adept at intervening elsewhere on a humanitarian pretext is suddenly inert. Why? I suspect the reason is that it has too much intervention on its plate already. The Burmese must die because we are too busy pretending to save Afghans and Iraqis. To such cynicism has liberal intervention sunk.

Burma was not alone in being denied the benefits of Western assistance. The plight of the people of Zimbabwe, many facing eviction and starvation under Robert Mugabe, was attracting widespread condemnation. He was reduced to offering food only to his party supporters.

Yet again interventionism held aloof. Why if it wished to rebut the charge of racism, did it turn a blind eye to Africa and Burma? We were back to the harder realpolitik of attacking countries only if they threatened our interest or offered a quick (or initially quick) pose to military story.

08.06.2008

ROBERT MUGABE'S decision to ban relief for his desperate citizens infringes every canon of human decency. It puts the Zimbabwean government – perhaps too dignified a term – beyond the regimes even of Burma and Sudan in callousness. The crude device of state food for votes is a direct challenge to world sympathy. It is a challenge to those who believe that such sympathy should be more than a collective cry of woe but should motivate action.

Zimbabwe is in chaos. People are uprooted, property confiscated, houses burnt, aid workers banned, opponents of the regime killed or mutilated and foreign diplomats arrested and their staff beaten. Morgan Tsvangirai [the opposition leader] is under rolling arrest. While the capacity of a subsistence economy to withstand collapse is always impressive, Zimbabwe is held back from mass starvation only by the flight of a quarter of its people beyond its borders.

Where now are the fine words of the international community in the Noble Nineties, boasting what Tony Blair called "the new doctrine of humanitarian intervention"? He declared in 1999 to rousing applause that the world order "could not turn its back" on flagrant "violations of human rights within other countries . . . Success is the only exit strategy I am prepared to consider."

We are older and wiser but the germ of a widely accepted idea remains. Today's world is indeed reluctant to stand by when large numbers of people are dying as a result of the deeds of alien regimes, however sovereign. It did not leave hundreds of thousands of Kurds, Kosovans or East Timorese to be driven from their homes or to their deaths. It mobilised opinion to aid them.

Even where the concept of such intervention was corrupted and abused, as in the invasions of Afghanistan and Iraq, it is to humanitarianism that apologists for these ventures still resort for justification. These countries must be occupied, they say, to save their people from a fate worse than self-determination. Humanity requires it.

Experts now reply that intervening in Darfur would be "logistically difficult". It would involve taking sides in what is essentially a civil war. That did not stop intervention in Kosovo. Experts say that in Burma intervention might have done more harm than good by alienating an already brutal regime. That did not stop us going into Somalia. Experts claim that Zimbabwe is really very complex, rooted in the politics of southern Africa and not our business. Such niceties did not impede the invasion of Afghanistan.

It may be that there is nothing we can do about the horrors of Darfur, Burma or Zimbabwe, or nothing that could make their plight any better. It may indeed be wiser to sit on our hands and leave it to our leaders to emit occasional howls of impotent contempt.

Yet the concept of humanitarian intervention, however limited, was sound. Willing coalitions should be able to enforce the relief of suffering where relief is feasible, as was surely the case in Burma. For the time being, the blood-soaked gutters of Baghdad and the poppy fields of Helmand have taken their toll.

If this seemed excessively gloomy, some action was taken against Zimbabwe, the worst action, the gesture diplomacy of trade sanctions. These were now advocated wherever intervention lacked the courage to send bombs or troops. They were imposed even where the victims of such sanctions, usually the poor, were innocent of

the crimes of their leaders and were impotent to reverse them or otherwise resist. Against a country that was already starving Britain proposed to make it starve even more. This to the policy of a modern "literal" government.

02.07.2008

THE SUPERMARKET group Tesco has decided to stop buying produce from Zimbabwe, "while the political crisis exists". Its competitor, Waitrose, has decided not to stop buying from Zimbabwe. It believes withdrawal would devastate "the workers and their extended families". They cannot both be right. They are not. Waitrose is right.

Economic sanctions is a coward's war. They do not work but are a way in which rich elites feel they are "committed" to some distant struggle. They enjoy lasting appeal to politicians because they cost them nothing and are rhetorically macho. They embody the spirit of "something must be done", the last refuge of stupidity in foreign policy.

Champions of economic sanctions can find hardly a shred of evidence in their favour, as indicated in the celebrated 1999 Congressional evidence of Richard Haas of Brookings. He was reduced to admitting they were a "blunt instrument that often produces unintentional and undesirable consequences".

Their first use in modern times, against Italy over Abyssinia in 1935, crashed the lira but did not free the Abyssinians. The USA's most ferocious sanctions drove Cuba into the arms of Russia and came near to precipitating a nuclear war – and cemented Castro in power. The same futility was seen in action against Russia, Poland, Rhodesia, Afghanistan, Nicaragua, Iraq and Iran.

Subjecting a political economy to siege leads to consequences. It enforces a command economy, in which the rulers keep what they want for themselves, skimming every deal and corrupting every transaction. It made Saddam Hussein the sixth richest man in the world, as it enriched the Taliban warlords, the Burmese generals and Robert Mugabe.

Sanctions over time destroy the mercantile, managerial and professional classes, the rootstock of opposition to totalitarian government. They push power into the hands of brute force. The withdrawal of trade closes factories, farms and mines, and debilitates the political effectiveness of those dependent on them. More people must rely on state handouts – that is, on the regime.

In almost every case, sanctions make the evil richer and more secure, and the poor poorer. What have they done for the Burmese or the Cubans? It was war that brought change, albeit chaotic, to Iraq and Afghanistan after sanctions had failed. South Africa was transformed not by sanctions but by the collapse of the moral coherence of Afrikanerdom, leading to an orderly transfer of power. It is arrogant for outsiders to claim any part in that remarkable process.

The only clear-cut case of a sanction working was America's sabotage of sterling during the 1956 Suez crisis. It was effective because Britain was a democracy whose government knew it could not survive a collapsing currency. This is the true paradox: to be susceptible to such pressure a state must have a government responsive to its people, but then such a government should not need sanctioning.

12

The Age of Endgames

A year and a half into the Baghdad surge and the extra troops were still on the ground in Iraq. But there was hope. In June 2008 Barack Obama emerged as the strongest Democrat candidate to fight the forthcoming presidential election. In a speech on 15 July he was emphatic: "I opposed the war in Iraq before it began, and would end it as president. I believed it was a grave mistake to allow ourselves to be distracted from the fight against al-Qaeda and the Taliban by invading a country that posed no imminent threat and had nothing to do with the 9/11 attacks. Since then, more than 4,000 Americans have died and we have spent nearly $1 trillion." He pledged he would leave, and fast. It was to prove easier said than done.

16.07.2008

THE SURGE in Iraq is much misread. It has involved pouring 20,000 extra troops into forward operating bases in central and western Baghdad, mostly Sunni areas. As a result, a formerly mixed city has been segregated into fortified enclaves as in Jerusalem and Belfast. Neighbourhoods have been flooded with armour, and soldiers embedded in each community. Not surprisingly, there has been a relative decline in lawlessness and violence, though they remain devastatingly high.

As long as the surge is judged by casualties, its success will be measurable. But assessment is confused because it coincides with a different innovation, the "awakening" in the Sunni Anbar province, initiated by the US marines a full year before the surge. It stimulated a shift in local power that has brought some stability to Sunni Iraq and diminished the running Shia–Sunni civil war.

In an extensive survey of withdrawal options in a recent issue of Foreign Affairs, the American Middle East analyst, Steven Simon, points out that the awakening resulted from a realisation on the part of Sunni tribal leaders that they were losing local control to incoming al-Qaeda units, who presented themselves as Sunni saviours against the Americans and Shia security forces.

Fed by a revulsion against al-Qaeda, Sunni leaders eventually turned to the Americans, who responded with money and weapons to the former Sunni militias. Known as "Sons of Iraq" they now number some 90,000. Fighters receive $360 a month and a local chief could earn $100,000 a year in skim for fielding a unit of 200 men. Some $200 million from American taxpayers vanished into Ramadi alone in just six months of 2007.

Such astronomical sums were not enough. Crucial to the Sunnis' change of tack was that they knew the Americans were leaving. They saw Washington moving towards the Democrats and withdrawal. "They talked about it all the time", recalls an American commander, also reported in Foreign Affairs, who told them: "We don't know when we are leaving, but we don't have much time."

Analysis in the latest Military Review concurs: "A growing concern that the US would leave Iraq and leave the Sunnis defenceless against al-Qaeda and the Iranian-supported militias made the younger leaders open to our overtures." In other words, while the surge yielded important reductions in crime, it was the "awakening" and its reading of American politics that was politically crucial.

The Iraq War was never going to end until Americans tired of it. Obama embodies that tiredness. He wants to send more troops to Afghanistan and has been told he cannot have two wars at once. Now he has a strategy for withdrawal, and evidence as to how it might work. The awakening remains high risk. Some see arming the militias as a reckless prelude to resumed civil war, while leaving Maliki to fend for himself might just see him fall.

Last year's British withdrawal from Basra, the segregation of Baghdad and the awakening in Anbar have shown that imminent withdrawal concentrates minds and shifts political plates. It has begun the partitioning of Iraq into self-securing provinces, and has formed power structures on which new leadership can be built. In this desperate country, still among the most dangerous on earth, disengagement's hour has come.

What I did not realise was the longer-term consequence of this policy of desperation, re-empowering the Sunni communities of Anbar and elsewhere. It supplied them with armed and organised militias ripe to oppose the hostile Shia rule of Baghdad, vulnerable to the sectarian blandishments of the Islamic State fanatics when they emerged in 2014.

If the humanitarian and "values" motives for intervention in Iraq had long worn thin, they were non-existent in Congo, probably the most dangerous country on earth. The International Red Cross estimated that over the previous decade some 5.4 million people had died in eastern Congo and the death toll was rising by some 45,000 a month. (These estimates were later disputed as exaggerated.) Yet Africa continued to exert a repelling magnet to Western interventionists.

05.11.2008

THE *GUARDIAN* headline was clear as mud. It read "Stop Killing in Congo or Else, Leaders Warned". Everything was left hanging. Which leaders? Warned by whom? Or else what? The story was that Western spokesmen had warned various African leaders, albeit via the press, that they would be "held to account, or else" if they did not do as they were told. This implied military intervention and there were briefings to that effect, though only a few hundred soldiers were mentioned.

These threats came from the new prophet of Blairite intervention, David Miliband, the foreign secretary, and from his French counterpart, Bernard Kouchner. On a media-drenched trip to Congo, both were in full megaphone mode. "The world is watching", they cried, as they peered into the impenetrable jungle. They went out on a limb and called for "an end to violence". Miliband's boss, Gordon Brown, intoned: "We must not allow Congo to become another Rwanda."

How does he propose to do that? The two countries whose history and military capacity most qualify them for "not allowing Congo" are Britain and the US. Both are fighting bitter and extravagant wars elsewhere. Their cost to British and American taxpayers is $3 trillion on the guesstimate of the American economist, Joseph Stiglitz. The idea that London or Washington – under whatever leadership – will send armies to Africa, to "or else" its leaders, is ludicrous. The 17,000 UN troops already there have been hopelessly overstretched.

Interventionists always ask their critics what they would do "instead". It is as if doing something counterproductive, or even just threatening it, must be better than doing nothing. This cannot be so. The new regime in Washington seems certain to pull back from the belligerent hubris of the Bush–Blair years. Explaining America's refusal to intervene after the Burma hurricane, its defence secretary, Robert Gates, appealed to "a greater sensitivity all over the world to violating a country's sovereignty". Yet he was about to drop drone bombs on Pakistan.

Congo's people cry out for world aid. Everything should be done to get food and shelter to those in need. No effort to that end is enough. But such help should be under the Red Cross rubric, that it should never wear uniform or travel under the shadow of a gun. We know that all aid has strategic import. It can harm as well as help. But charity is best when politically blind. It is born of humility and bravery, not empty bravado.

Obama took office in January 2009 and did as he promised, ordering a departure of American troops from Iraq and a review of NATO policy in Afghanistan. Both decisions were instantly surrounded with "issues". The American army had a terror of anything that might look like defeat, especially in Iraq. In Afghanistan the soldiers on the ground, most effective as special forces, were settling down to a new equilibrium. They held Kabul while the Taliban and other warlords wielded a turbulent power outside the capital.

25.03.2009

ONE WORD shines through the spin surrounding this week's Barack Obama policy review on Afghanistan. The word is exit. Before he became president, Obama was much taken by the idea that Afghanistan was a good and winnable war, a usefully macho contrast to his retreat from Iraq. But in a military briefing at the time, he asked what was the exit strategy from Kabul. He was met with silence. He got the point.

After nearly eight years of fighting, the original objective – to find Osama bin Laden – has eluded the strongest military coalition on earth, while liberal intervention is ever further from success in nation-building. Down south a British government has again sent an army to an unwinnable war against the Pashtuns. It never learns.

If Britain has forgotten, at least Obama appears to be learning from America's equivalent example, Vietnam. The drift to a repeat of that catastrophe is the last thing his presidency needs just now. He can see that the occupation of Afghanistan has made every mistake in the invader's handbook. It has been Vietnam for slow learners.

The Pentagon's use of the war to test its latest military kit, notably pilotless bombers, has been a disaster, ensuring that gains by soldiers on the ground are wiped out by aerial massacres that act as recruiting sergeants for the enemy. As for the anti-opium campaign, master minded since 2001 by the British, it was well described this week by Richard Holbrooke, Obama's "Af-Pak" aide, as "the most wasteful and ineffective programme I have seen in 40 years". It was little more than a Western subsidy to the Taliban.

Any long occupation by an invader eventually leads to a rough equilibrium of power, each component feeding the others. UN figures suggest that barely 10 per cent of outside aid reaching Afghanistan – including £1.6 billion from Britain – goes to its intended use. Most vanishes into the same power melting pot as the opium harvest and the Taliban's sources of cash in the Middle East.

The old maxims remain true: getting into a war is easy, getting out is hard. Obama seems to realise that the fate of America's Afghan adventure has come to depend not on what NATO does or does not achieve, but on the emergent Taliban and the stability of the shambolic regime in Pakistan's Islamabad. As previously with the Russians so with the West, this poor, intensely private country must one day see off another invader who sought to reorganise its history with guns, bombs and money. It has not worked. It was never going to work.

Whatever Obama wants, the Pentagon is clearly not going to leave Afghanistan as it fears it is leaving Iraq, with its tail between its legs. Advisers battle over whether to try an Iraq-style surge to

drive out the Taliban once and for all, or at least provide the American public with an appearance of victory. Or might there be some negotiations with the Taliban, whoever that is? Suddenly strategy thinks laterally, but finds only confusion and a hatred of defeat.

13.10.2009

THE ENDGAME begins, again. London waits on Washington. Washington waits on Barack Obama. Obama waits on Kabul. Kabul waits on history.

Reports from Washington suggest a battle royal is being fought, as happens at a turning point in every war. It is between the loss-cutters and the one-last-pushers. The cast is familiar. The soldiers, led by the third general in a year to guide America's Afghan War, Stanley McChrystal, are doing what soldiers always do. They are asking for more troops, either 40,000 more (a 60 per cent rise on the present American deployment) or preferably 80,000 more. This is coupled with our old friend, a "re-engineered" counter-insurgency strategy to win hearts and minds on the ground.

Some glimmers of sanity are showing in Washington, if not in London. Suddenly it is "time to negotiate with the Taliban", as if this were unthinkable before. There is talk of somehow separating Taliban from al-Qaeda, of good Taliban from bad Taliban, of decapitating the Taliban's extremist leadership with drone bombers.

There is even talk of the Taliban not being the real enemy of the West after all, as they keep asserting. Perhaps they are just colourful Pashtuns who mean no harm to anyone but each other. Their former hospitality to al-Qaeda was a phenomenon of the 1990s, which in future can best be prevented by means other than a regional war.

Enter those picadors, the historians, to taunt statesmen with darts of wisdom in their hour of torment. In America, debate over the future of the war has, according to recent reports, degenerated into an intriguing "battle of the books" on the precedent of Vietnam. Was defeat in south-east Asia the result of politicians refusing the army resources for one last surge, as claimed in Lewis Sorley's *A Better War*, or was it due to their losing control to the military, as claimed in Gordon Goldstein's *Lessons in Disaster*?

Needless to say, the Pentagon hawks are reading – and preaching – the former. They want an Iraq-style surge in Afghanistan to take, hold and pacify Taliban territory and eventually drive the insurgents back over the border into Pakistan. This would mirror what they believe would have happened in Vietnam after the 1968 Tet Offensive, had American public opinion not lost the will to continue the war.

The doves are reading Gordon Goldstein and demanding an urgent withdrawal to Kabul. Hamid Karzai's regime should be left to its fate by letting it negotiate with provincial warlords and the Taliban's local commanders, as it often claims it wants to do. The eventual outcome, as in Vietnam, would be a regime more tolerable to the West and more hostile to al-Qaeda.

In the event the Pentagon hawks won the short-term argument. A surge of 21,000 marines arrived, half of them to bolster Britain's desperately ailing expedition in Helmand, which the Americans had delegated to the British in 2006. At the time, British officers were contemptuous of the ineffectiveness of the Americans in taming Helmand. The Americans now returned the compliment in spades.

The place was a quagmire. Operations succeeded one another with ever fancier names: Achilles, Pickaxe Handle, Hammer, Sledgehammer Hit, Eagle's Eye, Red Dagger, Blue Sword, Panther's Claw, as if mere nomenclature was enough to scare the enemy. Over 300 British soldiers had died in the theatre. Ground taken one day would be lost the next, in the style of the Great War. Most painful was the July retreat from the hard-fought fortress of Sangin, a Taliban stronghold and centre of the opium trade. Britain had failed to stabilise it and in September Americans re-entered the ruined town.

Meanwhile in London in April a new coalition government took office under David Cameron. Unlike Obama he immediately indicated no change in policy on intervention. He could hardly do so, having supported every intervention of the previous decade. But Cameron did offer one hostage to fortune, setting up the Chilcot Inquiry into Tony Blair's conduct of the preliminaries to the Iraq war.

09.07.2010

As British troops retreat from the fortress of Sangin in south Afghanistan, a sleepy room in Westminster plays host to Chilcot. The British establishment is strangely dotty. Chilcot is like reviewing tactics at Passchendaele during the Battle of Britain, or Boudicca's charioteering during the charge of the Light Brigade.

Sangin should now, after three years of "hearts and minds", be safe in the hands of the Afghan army and police units. It is not, any more than is the rest of Helmand, the province allotted to British troops to pacify in summer 2006. Instead it is a forward operating base under perpetual siege, one that the Americans must abandon to the enemy or defend at battalion strength.

The Helmand fiasco was both predictable and predicted. When I spoke to the NATO commander, General David Richards, in Kabul in early June 2006, his blithe self-confidence was unnerving. He was about to implement the order of the then defence secretary, John Reid, to send 3,000 British troops south to "establish the preconditions for nation-building". Richards was dismissive of such US operations as Enduring Freedom and Mountain Thrust. They just bombed villages and recruited Taliban. He promised to win hearts and minds by "creating Malayan ink spots".

Those listening to Richards were incredulous. Had he heard or read nothing of the Pashtun, of their reputation as insurgents and their obsession with fighting anyone and everyone? We were airily waved aside as whingeing no-hopers. Britain would triumph because "the Afghans basically hate the Taliban". This was the time of Reid's notorious "not a shot fired" remark. It led to a woeful lack of troops, armoured cars and helicopters, and an appalling attrition rate of one in four soldiers killed or wounded.

Helmand has been a classic case of generals telling politicians what they want to hear. In three and a half years, 312 British soldiers have died as their exposed patrols offered nothing but target practice for the Taliban. Sangin, Musa Qala and Marjah are blazoned across Britain's front pages, not as victories but as hell-holes. The once-booming settlement of Sangin has reportedly been reduced to a squalid drugs entrepot and ghost town, like a battlefield which each side must keep recapturing to save face.

What is intriguing is no longer the catastrophe itself but rather how it came to pass. How did two democracies, operating in a climate of open debate, find themselves trapped in a decade of bloodshed, extravagance and mendacity? How did they accept the deaths of hundreds of their young men and thousands of non-combatant foreigners in a cause they could articulate only in cliches about democracy, security and female emancipation?

A stab at an answer comes in a book by Garry Wills, *Bomb Power: The Modern Presidency and the National Security State*. It was the advent of nuclear terror, according to Wills, that allowed democracies to grant their leaders extraordinary power to "push buttons", in effect to declare "one-man wars" without the customary deliberation.

Given that power, presidents (and prime ministers) abused it. Nixon could assert during Watergate that a crime, "when the president does it, is not a crime". Dick Cheney and George Bush could bring kidnap, detention, assassination and torture within the discretion of the "commander in chief". If domestic politics required it, the president would find and wage war. Cheney made eight trips to the CIA's headquarters to demand it prove a link between Iraq and 9/11. When evidence of Iraq WMD was not forthcoming, Cheney – like Tony Blair – simply asserted it: "There is no doubt that Saddam Hussein now has weapons of mass destruction."

We no longer need Chilcot to tell us that there was no shred of intellectual honesty in the claim that Iraq posed a military threat to the West. Yet the period is fast acquiring similarities with Weimar Germany. People knew what was happening but dared not say. The normal ramparts of democracy – courts, *habeas corpus*, civil liberty, freedom of speech, fearless intelligence – fell before "national security" as defined by a political cabal. Politics ceased to be the lubricant of democracy and became the source of its poison.

NATO's generals will eventually retreat to Kabul. There they will build a Baghdad-style "green zone" of fortifications and blast walls. The city will become a Western client statelet, floating on an ocean of corruption-fuelling dollars. It will last as long as liberal interventionists care to enjoy a lethal cocktail of incoming mortars and outgoing pie in the sky. When it is over, we shall have another Chilcot Inquiry.

In August 2010 the endgame in Iraq really did end with the departure of the last American combat troops. The country was now under the exclusive Shia leadership of Nouri al-Maliki, prime minister since 2006, and appeared to be heading for civil war, Shia against the Sunni minority. This time the West was not blackmailed into staying. It therefore seemed time to render some account for seven years of intervention in Iraq.

31.08.2010

YESTERDAY THE Iraq War was declared over by Barack Obama. As his troops return home, Iraqis are marginally freer than in 2003, and considerably less secure. Two million remain abroad as refugees, with another two million internally displaced. Ironically, almost all Iraqi Christians have had to flee. Under Western rule, production of oil – Iraq's staple product – is still below its pre-invasion level, and homes enjoy fewer hours of electricity.

The proper way to assess any war is not some crude "before and after" statistic, but to conjecture the consequence of it not taking place. Anti-Iraq hysteria began in 1998 with Bill Clinton's Operation Desert Fox, a three-day bombing of Iraq's military and civilian infrastructure, to punish Saddam for inhibiting UN weapons inspectors. Most independent analysis believed that Iraq had ceased any serious nuclear ambitions at the end of the first Iraq War in 1991, a view confirmed by investigators since 2003. Even so, Desert Fox was claimed to have "successfully degraded Iraq's ability to manufacture and use weapons of mass destruction". Whether or not this was true, there was no evidence that such an ability had recovered by 2003.

The Chilcot Inquiry has been swamped with stories of the American–British occupation on a par with William the Conqueror's "harrying of the north". That any twenty-first-century bureaucracy could behave with such cruel and bloodthirsty incompetence beggars belief. It was blinded by a conviction in its neo-imperial omnipotence. However much we delude ourselves, the West is still run by leaders, especially generals, drenched in the glory of past triumphs: leaders who refuse to believe that other nations have a right to order their own affairs. The awfulness of Iraq in 2003 was not so grotesque as to be our business, even had we been able to build the pro-Western, pro-Israeli, secular, capitalist utopia of neo-con fantasy.

The Iraq War will be seen by history as a catastrophe that did more than anything else to alienate the Atlantic powers from the rest of the world and disqualify them as global policemen. It was a wild overreaction by a paranoid, over-militarised American state to a single spectacular, but inconsequential, act of terrorism on 9/11. As such it illustrated how little international relations have advanced since the shooting of Archduke Ferdinand in Sarajevo. Its exponents are still blinded by incident.

13

Springtime in Libya

With Iraq "over" and Afghanistan on the wane, it was if the age of intervention had run out of steam. It needed some new cause to espouse. It soon found one. On 17 December 2010, a young Tunisian street trader committed suicide in public in protest of harassment by local officials. His action sparked the first revolution of the so-called Arab Spring. It was followed by street riots in Algeria, Oman, Yemen, Syria and Morocco. Then on 25 January the occupation of Tahrir Square in Cairo began. Egypt was bigger than all the others put together. The Arab Spring, through still winter, had come of age.

The international community greeted these protests with unashamed enthusiasm, but was unsure how to proceed. The uprisings seemed autonomous, mimicking each other but essentially local outpourings of domestic dissent. How might liberal interventionism respond to changes that appeared to be moving in the right direction but without external stimulus? In particular might intervention find a way to help events in Egypt, ruled by a regime so far regarded as friendly to the West yet sitting on a powder keg of 82 million Arabs?

02.02.2011

WE ARE hypocrites. We cheer on the brave Tunisians and Egyptians as they assert the revolutionary power of the street. Hands off, we cry. Let them do it their way. It has taken a long time, but let the people get the credit and be strengthened thereby. We gave no such licence to the Iraqis or Afghans. We presumed it was our job, not theirs, to dictate how they should be governed.

Hosni Mubarak of Egypt is another Saddam Hussein, a secular dictator ruling a Muslim country with a rod of iron through a kleptocracy of cronies. Less wealthy than Saddam, he has to rely on American support, but he was only a little more subtle in his ruthlessness.

We are told that there were sound strategic reasons for supporting Mubarak, as there once were for supporting Assad of Syria and Saddam himself. There were similar reasons for backing the Ben Ali dynasty in Tunisia and "Britain's good friend", the outrageous Colonel Gaddafi of Libya. All offered a supposed bulwark against Muslim extremism, a monster of which Americans and Britons are told to show a pathological, all-consuming and costly terror. Now apparently that no longer applies to Egypt.

In reality there is no such thing as an ethical foreign policy. There is something philosophical called ethics and something pragmatic called foreign policy. The art of diplomacy lies in navigating between them. The Blair/Bush "crusade for democracy" failed to do so.

Britain, with a history of ineptitude in handling Egypt, offered its pennyworth at the weekend. The Foreign Office said, "We don't want to see Egypt fall into the hands of extremists ... We want an orderly transition to free and fair elections, and a greater freedom and democracy in Egypt."

Who cares what Britain "wants" in Egypt? I imagine Egyptians want much the same in Britain but are not so arrogant as to say so. Egypt is not Britain's responsibility any more, in so far as it ever was. Egypt, Tunisia, Iran and Pakistan are all Muslim states wrestling with agonies of self-determination. The West's sole contribution has been to plunge two of their neighbours, Iraq and Afghanistan, into a blood-bath of insecurity and chaos. Asia is not our continent, these are not our countries and none of this is our business. We should leave them alone.

Through the first three months of the Arab Spring, Western intervention looked on with a mixture of excitement, awe and frustration. Finally in March 2011 it found its opportunity, in the sands of north Africa. Of all the uprisings, that which most attracted British attention was in Libya against Colonel Gaddafi. But he had been Tony Blair's "good friend" and apple in the eye of British oil companies and the London School of Economics. On whose side should Britain sit, that of an "Arab Spring" rebellion or on that of its ally?

There was no contest. A separatist revolt in Libya's second city of Benghazi offered David Cameron his Blair moment, a chance for a heroic intervention. But it was unclear what he meant to do. Some 14 NATO powers were prepared to join in a no-fly campaign, but was the objective to protect Benghazi's citizens against violent retribution from Tripoli, as initially stated, or take sides in an armed uprising designed to topple Gaddafi? On the example of Kosovo and elsewhere, that might take more than bombers.

09.03.2011

HAPPY DAYS are back for the sofa strategists and beltway bombardiers. After the miseries of Iraq and Afghanistan, a Libyan no-fly zone is the tonic they need. If you zero in from carrier A, you can take out the Tripoli air defences while carrier B zaps the mercenary bases and carrier C zooms in with Special Forces to secure the oilfields. You might tell the Americans to go easy on Leptis Magna after what they did to Babylon. Otherwise, let rip. You can sense the potency surging through Downing Street's veins. This is how wars begin, and beginning wars is politically sexy.

Libya strategists are said to be torturing themselves over timing. Barack Obama says he "needs" Gaddafi to go, and David Cameron's position is much the same. Why this need is so pressing when, just months ago, Gaddafi was a dear ally and patron of Western scholarship is a mystery. But in Cameron's statement on no-fly zones last week, Britain appeared to assert its right in international law to remove Gaddafi, as it did the Taliban and Saddam Hussein.

In this ambition it is supported by the leftwing international lawyer, Geoffrey Robertson, who claimed to have found a right for "states to render assistance to innocent civilians battling for their lives" wherever that might be. This right apparently "emerges or crystallises" not from any democratic decision but from "state practice, conventions, writings of jurists and dictates of collective conscience".

To this is added the bizarre claim that a "responsibility to protect" the underdog in a civil war "devolves on to the [UN] security council" and, if not, onto any Tom, Dick or Harry. In other words, military aggression is anything you can pay a lawyer to justify.

It is the Bush–Cheney theory of zero national sovereignty, and could be used to justify every aggressive war by Washington or Moscow over the last 50 years.

The legal cobbling-together of "rights" to justify military intervention is an invitation to global mayhem. But if Cameron has persuaded himself that Gaddafi must go because he is being beastly to his own people, what is he waiting for? Liberal intervention nowadays is self-legitimising and self-authorising. Why hold back? Libya is a tinpot country of just over six million people, within easy reach of air bases in Cyprus, Crete and Italy. Britain occupied Suez in a matter of days in 1956. The longer Britain and America wait, the more likely is Gaddafi to build his defences and win other Arabs over to resisting "Western imperialism".

The answer, of course, is that nobody wants to go that far as yet. Politicians want to "send a signal", offer vague support to rebels, and aid humanitarianism. There will be no mission creep. But what happens if the no-fly zone proves ineffective? It did not topple the Taliban or Saddam. That needed ground troops. Mission creep is the result of half-heartedness and imprecision in the initial stages of intervention. Eventually the aggressor is drawn into ground attack. Failure becomes "not an option", and a new nation must be built and expensively supported.

Libya was always going to be bloody one day. I find it incredible that Labour ministers, as they simpered in Gaddafi's presence, could have thought he would lie down like a lamb should his people rise against him. But unless we redefine words, he is not committing genocide and his brutality is hardly exceptional. If the rebels win it should be their victory, emerging from a new balance of power inside Libya. If they fail, they must fight another day. There is no good reason for us to intervene.

NATO's Libyan campaign began as a no-fly zone to protect Benghazi from Libya's air force. It quickly "crept" into a full-scale air bombardment in support of rebels in a civil war. By August 2011 this war was close to stalemate, with the bombing of Tripoli taking a severe toll in death and destruction. The rebels were sustained by British and other air-to-ground support, enough to stay in the field,

but not to win. I felt this was not a case for outside intervention, but if the West wished Gaddafi gone they should go in on the ground, as in Kosovo and Iraq, and get it over with. As it was we were war-keeping rather than peace-keeping.

03.08.2011

BRITAIN'S HALF-WAR against Libya is careering onward from reckless gesture to full-scale fiasco. As it reaches six months' duration, every sensibly pessimistic forecast has turned out true and every jingoistic boast false. Even if the desperate and probably illegal tactic of trying to assassinate Colonel Gaddafi gets lucky, Britain would find itself running a shambles of its own making, with troops having to go in to "keep the peace".

The Libyan rebels, portrayed by Whitehall propagandists as plucky little democrats, are hardly more sympathetic than Gaddafi's supporters, with those in the east at odds both with each other and with those in the West. While Britain claims to be "protecting" the population, the latest, admittedly unreliable, estimates put the civilian toll from bombing at 1,100 dead and countless injured. Certainly hundreds must have died. The allies are clearly running out of targets and must justify each new attack in terms more appropriate to a Maoist hysteric. Last week the Tripoli television station was destroyed and reporters killed, "to disrupt the broadcast of Gaddafi's murderous rhetoric". What has that to do with a no-fly zone?

Had David Cameron the courage of his convictions at the start and declared proper war on Gaddafi, we might be contemplating a Libyan spring. Why should we worry about Arab consent or UN support when we have had so little compunction about exceeding the Libyan mandate [simply to protect civilians]? The iron law of plunging into someone else's civil war is to choose the side most likely to win and make sure it does.

On 20 August rebel soldiers with the reported assistance of NATO special forces finally entered Tripoli. A week later Gaddafi's now ruined palace had fallen and he had fled. It was a costly and bloody intrusion by NATO but undoubtedly an instance of successful air power in support of a ground attack, albeit on a minor scale. It was the one military intervention in the Arab Spring. As such it was important that its legality be clear, the outcome be "democratic" and the rebels prove worthy of Western support. This was soon to prove an idle hope.

26.08.2011

NATO APPEARS to have toppled the Gaddafi regime in Libya to "liberate" its people. The days are over where the mere triumph of arms justifies itself. The rightness of a war and the honesty of its methods are vital if the new liberal interventionism is to carry its proclaimed moral clout. The Libyan operation is already being declared a classic success for the ideology. The following claims have been made for it over the past six months.

First, intervention was necessary to prevent a massacre in Benghazi. There had been no massacre in Benghazi, only the threat of an attack on the city by Gaddafi if the rebels failed to negotiate. While the threat was real, it was the sole basis on which UN and Arab league support was obtained for a no-fly zone. That threat was averted within days. No further resolution was gained to support a NATO advance on Tripoli.

The claim that the intervention "saved thousands of lives" was wholly conjectural, and must be set against the thousands that have certainly been lost, and may yet be lost, through the intervention. These deaths can be justified only on the thesis that any precipitated revolution is worth any number of lives.

The NATO pledge that there would be no foreign troops on the ground was mendacious. From the moment air power failed to achieve the undeclared goal of Tripoli's surrender, the pledge was broken. NATO ground troops were extensively deployed in Libya, the distinction between overt and covert forces being spurious. "Special" soldiers are still soldiers. Close air support is also identical in tactical effect to ground artillery, as deployed in the final assault on the Gaddafi compound.

Britain claimed it was not taking sides in a foreign civil war. It clearly was. The rescue of Benghazi mutated, as did the Iraq venture, into a wider war to remove a regime no longer to Britain's liking. Aid of every sort was given to the rebels, from political and diplomatic support to training, logistics and battlefield leadership in the attack on Tripoli.

Throughout the campaign, the British government has said it is "for the Libyan people to decide their own fate" and its involvement would end once a tyrant had departed the scene. That was naive. Britain has, with NATO, most emphatically decided the fate of the Libyan people. It has brought anarchy in the place of order, hoping that anarchy will be brief. It cannot disown the consequences.

The foreign secretary, William Hague, admitted as much this week. He declared: "We're not looking at British troops being a significant part of a stabilisation operation." Yet from the start of this operation, David Cameron knew that if he toppled Gaddafi, he would own the place. It was no good constantly saying he would "learn from Iraq". The lesson of Iraq was, don't do it in the first place.

In September Cameron paid a "victory" visit to Benghazi, but he did not dare set foot in Tripoli which by then was already too unsafe for any Western leader. They could no more walk the streets in "liberated" Baghdad. He had left Libya to the mercy of the triumphant rebels and the result was chaos. Over the following two years, brutalities worthy of Gaddafi were reported. Oil production slumped and Tripoli soon became a no-go area for outsiders. By the summer of 2014, the British embassy had to close. Libya was no longer on the interventionist's map. It was no longer news.

With Libya out of the way, what still of Iran? Might it be induced to join the Arab Spring? That Iranians are not Arabs was a subtlety lost on latter-day interventionism. The scene now moved to that most hysterical of political theatres, an American presidential election. Barak Obama had already signaled retreat from Iraq and Afghanistan. Was there somewhere elsewhere the Republicans could accuse him of being weak?

04.11.2011

THIS TIME there will be no excuses. Plans for British support for an American assault on Iran, revealed in yesterday's *Guardian*, are appalling. They would risk what even the "wars of 9/11" did not bring: a Christian–Muslim Armageddon engulfing an entire region. No one should say they were not warned, that minds were elsewhere, that we were told it would be swift and surgical.

To Western strategists, Iran today is where Iraq was in 2002. The country posed no threat to the West, yet "weapons of mass destruction" were said to be primed and had to be urgently eliminated. The offending regime could be subjugated by air power or, if not, by regime change. The cause was noble, and the outcome sure.

There any comparison ends. Iran is not a one-man, two-bit dictatorship, but a nation of 70 million people, an ancient and proud civilisation with a developed civil society and a modicum of pluralist democracy. Certainly its insecure leader, Mahmoud Ahmadinejad, wants a weapons-ready nuclear enrichment programme, as next week's United Nations report by the International Atomic Energy Authority is expected to repeat. But he leads a country which, like Pakistan, Britain or Israel, craves prestige and the vague security that these unusable weapons seem to convey.

Nuclear dissemination is deplorable, but massively overhyped. Warheads cost a fortune to develop and keep in service. Nuclear bombs have not made Israel more secure. They have been useless to Pakistan in confronting India, and to North Korea against the south. They did not save apartheid in South Africa, or the Soviet Union from itself. Anti-Western aggression finds it cheaper and more effective to use terrorist outrages.

If ever there were a country once ripe for soft-power diplomacy, it was modern Iran. Yet the West misread Ahmadinejad and then misread such dissenters as Mohammad Khatami and parliament's speaker, Mehdi Karroubi. It defied pleas from moderates not to impose sanctions, rejecting the argument that Iran needed a strengthened professional, commercial and academic class as counterweight to the military and the mullahs. As with the sanctions imposed on Saddam's Iraq, Gaddafi's Libya and Mugabe's Zimbabwe, they have driven Iran's rulers into a siege economy.

Anyone watching last month's Republican primary debate in Las Vegas will have been shocked at the belligerence shown by the six candidates towards the outside world. It was a display of what the historian Robert D Kaplan called "the warrior politics … of an imperial reality that dominates our foreign policy". The spectacle was frightening and depressing. British friends of America can see all the signs of another country in the throes of "losing an empire and not finding a role", of a paranoid nervous breakdown. Britain has been there before. It should never go back.

14

Aftermath: Syria, Yemen, Mali, Ukraine

In the course of 2012 the Arab Spring was starting to look sickly. The Egyptian people returned to the streets to demand the military government give way to elections, which in June led to a victory for the Islamist government of the Muslim Brotherhood. Protests in Syria escalated into open conflict, leading to attacks on Homs and widespread killing of dissidents by the government of Bashar al-Assad. In July, Syria was declared to be in a state of civil war with atrocities committed on both sides. Could the West stand idly by?

20.07.2012

A YEAR ago the Syrian regime was "on the brink of collapse". Following the Houla massacre in May, President Assad was "on his way out". Now his opponents have reached the streets of Damascus and Aleppo, and it is "the beginning of the end for Assad". To Britain he is "unacceptable", to America brutal and bloodthirsty, to the United Nations the architect of "civil war". The language of international affairs seems unable to handle the morass of horror, damnation, reporting bias and wish fulfillment that overwhelms these half-understood conflicts. The task of analysis falls to the gods of cliche.

Lovers of Syria hope that its people can escape their present agony. Surrounded by torment in Iraq, Lebanon and Israel–Palestine, Damascus has seemed a haven of relative stability and tolerance. It has received two million refugees from Iraq's ongoing war, including virtually all its Christians. But hoping is rarely enough. For a quarter of a century the West's political instinct has been to crave action. Taxpayers who have spent billions on armies cannot see why they must sit and watch death and destruction on television when they believe they have the means to stop it.

Some Syrian opposition groups clearly think the same. They saw brave insurgents with noble causes suck Western troops into regime change in Somalia, Kosovo, Iraq and Afghanistan. The Arab spring failed to topple the Assad regime which, for all its faults, many Syrians still regarded as a guardian of stability. Could outsiders not do for Syria's insurgents what they did for Gaddafi's opponents in Libya?

The answer has been no. America and NATO are exhausted by ill-judged and expensive interventions, even where they have succeeded in toppling rulers. The most valid revolutions have proved to be home-grown and home-won, as in Tunisia and Egypt. A foreign footprint on Syrian soil would weaken the legitimacy of whoever or whatever follows Assad. New rulers seem stronger if they gain power through a resolution of internal forces rather than with the overt aid of a foreign power.

That is plain. What is less so is how a West sated on intervention can calibrate its response to these crises. What of Yemen, Mali, Congo or perhaps even the Gulf? Western diplomacy seems to know no middle ground between war and the vacuity of rhetoric. The reason for intervening in Libya but not in Egypt or Syria was opportunistic. Now the West appears to be executing a U-turn towards non-intervention. This is welcome. But the language of engagement or disengagement must follow suit.

Just as the costs and complexities of armed intervention were becoming prohibitive, technology supplied it with an ostensibly exciting new weapon, the pilotless long-distance drone. It gave an aggressor with access to airfields power to drop bombs with impunity almost anywhere on earth. Eleven countries already had them in their arsenals, unconcerned by any challenge to their legality or morality. Already America was using them against Taliban in southern Pakistan and against al-Qaeda "affiliates" in Yemen. I wondered if an aggressive weapon that was stripped of the encumbrance of invasion and occupation would breathe new confidence into the age of intervention. But what had it to do with bringing humanitarian relief?

10.01.2013

THE GREATEST threat to world peace is not from nuclear weapons and their possible proliferation. It is from drones and their certain proliferation. Nuclear bombs are useless, prestige playthings for the powerful. It is drones that are sweeping the global arms market. There are some 10,000 said to be in service, of which a thousand are armed and mostly American. Some reports say they have already killed more civilians than died in 9/11.

I have not read one independent study of the drone wars in Afghanistan, Pakistan and the horn of Africa that suggests they serve any strategic purpose. Their "success" is expressed solely in body count, the number of "al-Qaeda-linked commanders" killed. If dead bodies meant victory, the Germans would have won Stalingrad and the Americans Vietnam.

Neither the legality nor the ethics of drone attacks bears examination. Last year's exhaustive report by a group of Stanford and New York lawyers concluded they most were illegal, killed civilians, and were militarily counter-productive [*Henry L. Stimson Center and joint report by Stanford Law School and New York University School of Law*]. The report unequivocally concluded, "The United States should not conduct a long-term killing program based on secret rationales." John B Bellinger III, former counsel to the NSC and Jeff Smith, former counsel to the CIA, declared that drones were not consistent with "more basic rule-of-law principles that are at the core of the American identity and that we seek to promote around the world". Among the already reported deaths were an estimated 176 children. Such slaughter would have an infantry unit court-martialled and its generals sacked.

This week President Obama appointed two drone supporters, Chuck Hagel and John Brennan, as his defence secretary and CIA chief respectively. The military-industrial complex is licking its lips. If Obama, himself a lawyer, had any reservations about the legality of these weapons, he has clearly overcome them.

Since the drone war began in earnest in 2008, there has been no decline in Taliban or al-Qaeda performance attributable to it. The Afghan president, Hamid Karzai, has called the attacks "in no way justifiable". The Pakistan government, at whose territory they are increasingly directed, has withdrawn all permission.

The young Yemeni writer Ibrahim Mothana protested in the *New York Times* of the carnage drones are wreaking on the politics of his country, erasing "years of progress and trust-building with tribes". Yemenis now face al-Qaeda recruiters waving pictures of drone-butchered women and children in their faces. Notional membership of al-Qaeda in Yemen is reported to have grown by three times since 2009. Jimmy Carter declares that "America's violation of international human rights abets our enemies and alienates our friends".

The tenuous legality of this form of combat requires the aggressor to have "declared war" on another state. But al-Qaeda is no state. As a result these attacks on foreign soil are not just wars of choice, they are wars of invention. How soon will it be before the US declares itself "at war" with Iran and Syria, and sends over the drones? When it does, and the killing starts, it can hardly complain when the victims retaliate with suicide bombers.

Nor will it just be suicide bombers. Drones are cheap and will easily proliferate. The US is selling them to Japan to help against China. China is building 11 bases for its Anjian drones along its coast. The Pentagon is now training more drone operators than pilots. What happens when every nation with an air force does likewise, and every combustible border is buzzing with them?

When they were called guided missiles, drones were in some degree governed by international law and protocol. Obama rejects all that. He is teaching the world that a pilotless aircraft is a self-justifying, self-exonerating, legal and effective weapon of unilateral war. However counter-productive a drone may be, it cuts a glamorous dash on the home front. It is hard to imagine a greater danger to world peace.

A side-effect of the post-intervention anarchy in Libya in 2011 was a flood of weapons passing into the hands of Islamist militants across the Sahara, notably in the unstable former French colony of Mali. One group succeeded in capturing the desert city of Timbuktu. France offered aid to the Malian regime in retaking it. The British Cabinet was captivated at the "foreign legion" image of a desert

intervention and eagerly sought involvement. It seemed oblivious of the irony that the collapse of law and order in Mali was a direct spin-off of British intervention in Libya. In the event Timbuktu was quickly recaptured without the aid of British troops. Mission creep was never allowed to leave its starting block.

30.01.2013

JUST A week ago David Cameron clearly indicated there would be "no boots on the ground" in Mali. His office declared there was "absolutely" no question of British troops entering the conflict "in a combat role". Britain would lend two C-17 transports and that was it. To this was soon added a surveillance plane. Now there is to be a roll-on-roll-off ferry. As French troops advanced on Timbuktu, the adrenaline of triumph drifted across the Channel and into the nostrils of Westminster.

Cameron descended into his Cobra bunker, his lips quivering with the thrill of fear. Like every prime minister who uses that place, he emerged feeling he had to talk Churchill. He told the Commons: "We must frustrate the terrorists with our security. We must beat them militarily. We must address the poisonous narrative they feed on. We must close down the ungoverned space in which they thrive, and we must deal with the grievances they use to garner support." The most delicious word here was we.

Africa still echoes to the drum of empire. European powers are drawn back to redefine and reclaim their old responsibilities. Mali is France's Sierra Leone. To pretend that it poses an "existential threat" to Britain passes belief. Cameron has to elevate the supposed Malian "affiliates" of al-Qaeda to the status of a "generational" menace, which he claims will last for decades. They must be "beaten militarily", "the ungoverned space" in which they thrive must be "closed down" and the grievances on which they prey must be dealt with. And all by us.

There is no remit under the UN or international law for Britons to be fighting wars in the Sahara. We grasp at the fact that we are an EU ally of France, which is an ally of the part of Mali that failed to protect its northern citizens from marauding gangsters. It is odd how eager Cameron is to cite the EU when on shaky ground.

In yesterday's *Guardian* the al-Qaeda historian Jason Burke gave a detailed assessment of that movement's current condition. It bore not the slightest relation to the global monster of the prime minister's Cobra-fevered imagination. It was not on the same planet. Even at its height a decade ago, al-Qaeda could do no more than sponsor a few terrorist spectaculars. These were nasty, but modern cities can survive them, and modern policing appears recently to have their measure.

Al-Qaida has failed to win over a government, a territory or a large body of support. If it (whatever it is) really planned the Mali incursion, it could not even hold Timbuktu. Cameron's politics of fear may be in need of an enemy, but is this the best he can do to stir the blood of the heirs of Blenheim and Waterloo? Mali in practice may prove no big deal. It is Mali in theory that is dangerous.

The toughest test for Arab Spring interventionists was to be Syria. Initial predictions that the Assad regime would go the way of the rulers of Tunisia, Egypt and Libya proved predictably false. The designation of Assad's opponents as "good guys" worthy of Western support crumbled into implausibility as opposition factions fragmented and some fell under the influence of Islamist extremists, some even more fanatical than al-Qaeda. The civil war became that interventionist's nightmare, complicated.

In London David Cameron, trailing Labour in the polls, craved another Libya. He dived into Cobra. Meetings with military advisers examined options. There was talk of "remember Benghazi, remember Srebrenica". Then on 30 August the House of Commons delivered the prime minister a humiliating snub, denying him freedom to bomb Syria and forcing him to promise he would not do so. Instead Russia, Assad's long-time backer, was drawn into the fray, securing Assad's promise to dismantle his chemical weapons arsenal.

18.09.2013

THE DARK curtain draws back and over the blood-stained stage flutters a small white dove. Some twist of war has sent it aloft. Some missile roar may soon bring it crashing to Earth. But while its wings still flap, we gaze at it mesmerised by hope.

Syria is now the war game of choice among the armchair strategists of Washington and London. Cynics battle with optimists, belligerents with pacifists. Has Barack Obama been painted into a corner? What if Assad pulls back and Russia vetoes a military response? Has America's bluff been called?

The greatest fallacy of all is a belief that the power, the knowledge and the legitimacy of the international community are enshrined in some Anglo-American suzerainty. The UN doctrine of responsibility to protect was a concept noble in the drawing rooms of Manhattan, but it has degenerated into an excuse for more bloodshed. It has become a diplomatic Babel of grandstanding, warmongering, neo-imperialism and general half-heartedness. Its signatures are the missile strike and the punitive sanction.

Syria's civil war is as horrible as any. It is rooted in a religious feud that baffles most outsiders and seems as vicious as anything inflicted on Europe by the Thirty Years war. "You may find some of these images distressing," the BBC announcer intones each night, before another orgy of propaganda for the "do something" and "don't stand idly by" lobby.

It stands to the credit of legislators on both sides of the Atlantic that they have resisted this propaganda. They have challenged their leaders to say what purpose is served by merely bombing dictators. To them, war with Syria should be explained not just asserted. It has nothing to do with America "reverting to isolation" or Britain as "an offshore island". It has to do with common sense, with not doing more harm than good.

A deal with Russia on chemical weapons in Syria could yet morph into the most plausible route to peace, a ceasefire and some de facto partition. This could be a prelude to a return of refugees and relief to the region generally. Were it to lead on to a deal on nuclear weapons with Iran, it would be an added bonus.

Even as the interventionist tide appeared to be receding over the course of 2014, its shortcomings were spot-lit by the new Russian belligerence towards the east European state of Ukraine. This was

seized on as a classic illustration of the need for intervention, yet a need lacking a means of implementation. The old Cold War drum could be taken from its closet and beaten, but so what? The West was not going to war with Russia. That was inconceivable. Instead the belligerence was used by the defence lobby to plead for an increase in spending and a replenishing of Cold War arsenals. In the van was the veteran American defence secretary Robert Gates on a visit to London in January 2014.

17.01.2014

SURPRISE, SURPRISE. A defence secretary thinks more should be spent on defence. The former Pentagon boss Robert Gates is in Britain promoting his old lobby and his new book. He is concerned that Britain's current defence cuts may deprive the Atlantic alliance of "full-spectrum capabilities". They will weaken the world's fourth largest armed force (Britain's, believe it or not) in deterring dreaded foes. The chancellor of the Exchequer George Osborne is supposed to shake in his shoes.

Gates claims to be horrified by Barack Obama's micromanagement of America's wars. The advent of modern surveillance and drone technology means that, "for too many people ... war has become a kind of video game", he says, professing himself "even more sceptical of systems analysis, computer models, game theories and doctrines that suggest that war is anything other than tragic, inefficient and uncertain".

I occasionally attend defence seminars to immerse myself in their exotic surrealism. A recent one comprised soldiers, think-tankers and arms suppliers, all living off the public purse. They were like Macbeth's witches, incanting: "By the pricking of my thumbs/ Something wicked this way comes", before stirring quantities of taxpayers' money into their brew. "Thrice to thine and thrice to mine/ And thrice again, to make up nine", they chant, the nine being billions, not millions.

No one at these events ever talks about who is being defended against whom. We are just warned that if the defence lobby does not get its money, "capabilities will degenerate" and allies desert. Assorted so-called "wars", on terror, drugs, human traffickers or whatever, will be lost. The Ministry of Defence is like *Benefits Street* [a current television series about people living on welfare] but for slow learners.

Without some idea of an enemy, we cannot judge how much defence is needed where. Not since the end of the Cold War has there been a sensible threat to Britain. The defence lobby converts criminal deeds by terrorists into threats to "national security". The truth is that, other than the bizarre post-imperial Falklands War, every foreign conflict to which British troops have been committed in modern times has been not defensive but aggressive. It is aggression on which we currently spend £40 billion a year.

Gates maintains that today's threats are as dangerous as during the Cold War, coming from the Middle East and Asia generally. I know of no states that pose even the remotest threat to the UK or Europe, let alone one liked to be deterred by armies, navies and air forces or by nuclear missiles. A few hot-headed terrorists may threaten dire deeds, but rarely more than bomb blasts. These are matters for the police and security services, whom God preserve.

The reality is that the devil makes work for idle hands. The drone wars that the US and Britain are waging across the Muslim world have become test-beds for the makers of these dreadful weapons. Armed forces sit champing at the bit. Defence industries gasp for money. Belligerents demand that "something be done" in Syria or wherever. Perhaps Ministry of Defence has become a misnomer. It should be renamed the Ministry of Attack.

A godsend came to the aid of Gates and his allies in the form of Russia's occupation in February 2014 of the Ukrainian enclave of Crimea, which formerly belonged to Russia. It was an act of aggression against the territory of a state newly befriended by the West. But the majority wishes of the Crimean people were clearly for Russia. It was a repeat of the self-determination by which the interventionists set such store in Kurdistan and Kosovo. However, for the first time in the age of intervention the West confronted an enemy far beyond its capacity to confront militarily, let alone defeat. London and Washington could do little but froth at the mouth.

12.03.2014

AT LEAST the West is agreed on what must be done to stop Russia's reoccupation of Crimea. It agrees that nothing can be done. Paradox is the stuff of foreign policy. It produces summits, holds conferences, forms and reforms contact groups. Leaders make interminable phone calls and think-tanks rush joyfully to club class lounges. Everywhere something must be done and nothing can be done. Must fights can.

On Monday night I visited a Ukraine seminar in Westminster. It was crammed with diplomats, defence experts and pundits and was a somber occasion. The understand-Russia tribe argued with the understand-Ukraine tribe. Stand-firmers fought realpolitikers. Putin's bombast was pitted against Putin's paranoia. The West's righteous indignation was pitted against its double standards. Yet all agreed on one thing. Something must be done.

It was not really a seminar on Ukraine at all, it was a meeting of the global trade union of "something-must-be-doners". Participants seemed liberated by the impossibility of driving Putin from Crimea by force. Hence we enjoyed a cold buffet of messages, warnings, deterrents, red lines, sanctions, gestures, carrots and sticks. Barack Obama "must not appear weak". NATO must "give a clear signal". The EU must appear united.

Russia's occupation of Crimea may or may not reflect Putin's paranoia at the West's muscle-flexing along its border. Kiev's fight for independence may or may not reflect a justified fear of Russian revanchism. I do not know. I know only that neither country threatens us, and neither "belongs to us". Some people just cannot bear to be left out of a fight.

Russia remained in possession of Crimea as Western sanctions bit on its financial sector and on the notorious "oligarchs" around Putin. In return he imposed trade bans on European goods, much to the discomfort of many German and Polish merchants. Soon afterwards, a new separatist movement developed in eastern Ukraine. Again the driver was Russian-speaking districts hostile to the new regime in Kiev. Clear Russian involvement in the uprising was again met with

a deluge of abuse from the West, but not much else. Even the accidental shooting down of a Malaysian airliner, apparently with a Russian missile, did not dent Russia's support for the dissidents. There was nothing the West could or would do about it.

At this point a black cloud of nemesis seemed to gather round the heads of Western leaders. Russia shrugged off sanctions, Syria's Assad seemed impregnable and the Taliban opened offices in Gulf capitals. Then Iraq returned to haunt Washington and London. A group of extremists called the Islamic State (IS) emerged from the chaos of northern Syria to invade Iraq as far as the Kurdistan border. They brought with them a peculiar savagery against "non-believers", notably any non-Sunnis.

Governments in Damascus, Baghdad and Kurdistan seemed powerless to resist IS. Mosul and Fallujah fell, as did the Sunni Anbar province. IS troops advanced almost to the suburbs of Baghdad. This was a grotesque outcome of the Coalition's decade of intervention in Iraq. Nothing so clearly indicated that such adventurism was coming to an end than the West's reaction to the truly ghostly rise of IS.

22.08.2014

DAVID CAMERON wants Britain to stay out of Iraq. "We are not going to get involved", he says, "No boots on the ground ... no sending in the British army." Assuming he means it, he is right. He is right to focus Britain's response to the Islamic State on humanitarian aid. He is right not to abandon his holiday, which would merely suggest that Iraq is Britain's responsibility.

Iraq today is not easy for non-interventionists. In a real sense it is a British responsibility. We helped smash it. We created the mess and therefore "owned it". Without any legal justification, we toppled and killed Iraq's ruler, Saddam Hussein. We sent home his army and dismantled law and order. We broke the ruling party and civil service, causing the chaos that exiled the middle classes and massacred tens of thousands of civilians. We still dare not even to publish the Chilcot report which might say we did all this.

Yet to be responsible for a mistake does not imply the capacity to correct it. Throughout the age of intervention, the West almost always was on the side of rebellion against an established regime: Kosovans against Belgrade, northern tribes against Kabul, Shi'a against Saddam, Benghazi against Tripoli. Interventionists claimed to be for freedom against tyranny, but were mostly for chaos against order.

Iraq now desperately needs the world's humanitarian aid, and this is rightly forthcoming. But what of the need that breeds the need? Baghdad's army faces a deadly foe. Whatever past faults may have given rise to IS, 10 years ago the West went to war for the sake of a better Iraq. Should it not do so again if any shred of benefit from that occupation is to survive?

The sole answer is air power, fool's gold of intervention-lite. Bombing sounds macho, looks good on television and "destroys convoys". It appeals to the techno-nerds of the arms business, with their drones. But bombs are never accurate. IS may be cynical in claiming to kill hostages only in revenge for deaths from American bombs, but drones give it that excuse.

Close air support for ground troops in open country played a useful part in recent wars, such as the rebel advances on Kabul and Tripoli. It may take out a few IS tanks. But the "strategic" role of air power is mere air force propaganda. The idea that bombing can turn a war is folly. There is no reason to think that Western bombs will restore the fortunes of the Iraqi government or force IS to admit defeat. IS will be defeated politically only in the hearts and minds of the Sunni populations of Syria and Iraq. This is no computer war game.

If Britain really feels historic guilt over the 2003 invasion, then it should do what it did in Kosovo and Afghanistan and originally in Iraq. It should fight alongside the new Iraqi prime minister, Haider al-Abadi. It should reconquer and occupy territory and defend its border. IS would be driven back into Syria where Assad would have to finish it off. Perhaps the Russians and the Iranians could be induced to help. London could then resume "nation-building" in Baghdad. This is, of course, barking mad.

Cameron was silly to claim this week, in a welter of *Sunday Telegraph* platitudes, that ISIS was "a danger to Europe", that its caliphate was "not miles from home" and threatened "the brighter future we long for". He should sprinkle something else on his cornflakes. Both he and Obama have denied any intention to reoccupy Iraq. Public opinion will never allow it. The belligerence that fills every newscast and media outlet is merely giving IS street cred in fighting the great Satan. It is to such tub-thumping opportunism that the twenty-first century's interventionism has been reduced.

The response in Britain to the advance of IS in Iraq and Syria was a true interventionist hangover. Given the atrocities perpetrated by IS there was no doubt that a humanitarian intervention was legitimate. The UN was appalled. Everyone yearned for something to be done. But populations exhausted by military action refused to contemplate further invasions. As a result, no one had the first idea what might help the victims of IS on the ground. Politicians were stumbling all over the shop.

10.10.2014

I CANNOT recall a war so swamped in incoherent response as that in Iraq. The awfulness of IS has given intervention a clear moral imperative. David Cameron's party conference speech frothed with "evil people, pure and simple". It dripped with killed children, raped women, genocides and beheadings. The prime minister declared that "some people seem to think we can opt out of this. We can't. There is no walk-on-by option."

Cameron then walked on by. He suggested that a bit of bombing would do the trick while conceding that "the troops on the frontline" would be "Iraqis, Kurds and Syrians fighting for the safe and democratic future they deserve". None would be British. The adjectives were apocalyptic, the response cosmetic.

The same is true in America. Barack Obama may have been elected on a platform of withdrawal from foreign wars, but he too must scamper from helicopter to White House dodging jibes of impotence. His plea that "doing stupid stuff" is no answer to a global crisis is derided by his old secretary of state, Hillary Clinton. "Great nations need organising principles", she says, whatever they may be. "Not doing stupid" lacks what the *New Yorker* last month called the "snarl and swagger" that Americans want in their leaders.

That war has all the best tunes is a truism. So is the relief that governments in trouble have long drawn from foreign adventures and manufactured foreign threats. Cameron is emerging as a typical politician of fear, with his hyperbolic elevation of IS as a menace that "we must deal with or they will deal with us, bringing terror and murder to our streets". An inability to differentiate between lethal criminality and national security is dangerous in a democratic leader.

Britain's strategy is now to howl blue murder and then declare a sort of half-war. A conflict we have neither the intention nor the capacity to end, and that should be contained regionally, is internationalised. We bequeathed to a bunch of warrior zealots an anarchic nation and a vast arsenal to play with. Their victims desperately need our aid, as do the victims of war everywhere, but not our bombs. For the price of a bombed pick-up truck you could feed a refugee camp for a year.

By the winter of 2014 IS was cementing its hold on the towns and cities of a swathe of Syria and Iraq. It looked probable that in time the relevant governments and their armies would push them back. But evidence of support from Sunnis exasperated at the exclusive policies of Damascus and Baghdad suggested this would be a long process. The increased role of Shiʻa Iran in helping Iraq fight IS further complicated Western strategy.

My prediction of a partitioned Iraq looked more and more likely. As in Yugoslavia, Afghanistan and Libya the consequence of intervention was almost always the break-up of nation states into smaller ones. It was a strange legacy. But by 2014 intervention was tired and exasperated at its own failings. It had lost public support. The horrors of the IS were to prove its demise – for the time being.

Epilogue

As the age of intervention appeared to be drawing to a close, America, Britain and their allies were again plunged into agonising over how to meet another humanitarian catastrophe, this one partly of their own making. The menace of the warlords of the Islamist State in Syria and Iraq was worse than anything posed by the Taliban, Saddam Hussein or Muammar Gaddafi. Yet there was no appetite for armed intervention. American and British leaders were emphatic on this point. Their nations were exhausted by war. They would utter rhetorical damnation and drop an occasional bomb, but no more "feet on the ground".

Two decades of intervention had delivered seven wars, two in Iraq, two in former Yugoslavia, one each in Afghanistan, Sierra Leone and Libya. Two of these, in Afghanistan and Iraq, were more protracted than any seen in the twentieth century. Few lessons were learned from each. Invasions were planned but not occupations, which were often chaotic. The world's most powerful armies found themselves humbled by the world's most primitive. The expense was colossal, some \$3–4 trillion on one estimate,[1] the benefits largely elusive. At the end there was a ghost of democracy in Afghanistan and Iraq, but little stability, peace or prosperity. None of the "victorious powers" dared walk the streets in the capitals they claimed to have freed from oppression.

Britain had no "dog in the fight" of any of these wars. Its national security and its economic well-being were never at risk. Yet it was party to the partitioning of Yugoslavia, and the creation of Bosnia and Kosovo as heavily subsidised European protectorates. It rendered Sierra Leone's government permanently dependent on the British army. In the process two large Asian nations, Iran and Pakistan, were destabilised.

---

[1] Stiglitz and Bilmes, *The Trillion Dollar War: The Trul Cost of the Iraq Conflict*, 2008.

The Arab Spring of 2011 erupted, collapsed and then reverted to the status quo ante, grim in Egypt, terrifying in Syria. Israel's security and its relationship with Palestine remained in a state of trauma.

Far from having protected themselves or the world from terrorism, countries such as America and Britain professed themselves more threatened by it than ever. There were new restrictions on civil liberty. Relations with Muslim populations across Europe deteriorated, alongside an upsurge in antagonism to the flows of immigrants fleeing the wars. London was soon playing host to unprecedented numbers of supposedly liberated Kosovans, Afghans, Iraqis and Libyans.

I wrote sceptically of these interventions throughout the period. Since most, though not all, turned out to be disasters, I felt vindicated. But there were predictions I got wrong. All observers want to see their preconceptions validated, and this can colour judgment of what was and was not appropriate for intervention.

Most of my reservations were over the preliminaries to conflict, especially the ready resort to bombing as a humanitarian tool and proxy for war. I initially opposed Kosovo because I could not see how bombing Belgrade was remotely likely to end ethnic cleansing in Kosovo. Only a land army, or at least a threat of one, would work. This eventually proved to be the case, though I was also wrong to think this might be a "hot" war.

I was right about Afghanistan and Iraq, but wrong initially about Libya. I took the view that intervention in Libya by bombing alone would merely prolong a civil war. I also thought probably the rebellion would not succeed, whether or not we were right to take sides in it. As it turned out, bombing in support of the rebel army and with special forces on the ground did topple Gaddafi. The intervention concluded in what is a catastrophe for Libya and its people, but that could not have been predicted at the time.

A more important reflection on motive. When nations go to war on other nations, the question of intent is naturally uppermost. The motives for the age of intervention were obscure, tending to shift as circumstances changed on the ground. The result was seriously to compromise the morality of intervention as such and, in my view, to vitiate its purpose.

The initial objective was humanitarian, to stop ethnic cleansing in Bosnia and Kosovo. The urge to aid those in distress had soared with the end of the Cold War and the relaxing of the UN's adherence to respect for state sovereignty. Man's capacity for inhumanity had not, as far as I can tell, increased, but the willingness to combat it had done so. What was formerly an essentially "pacifist" response – witness the intervention in the Ethiopian famine in the 1990s – was now militarised. The desire to "do something" became a desire to do almost anything.

Bosnia and Kosovo were ostensibly successful interventions. Even here the dismantling of a rudimentary democracy by outside force was drastic. In addition the intervention to assist Bosnia's Muslim revolt was a direct invitation to Kosovo's dissidents – previously cast as terrorists by America – to play the same card. This raised what Oxford's professor of international relations, Jennifer Welsh, calls the "moral hazard of the new interventionism". She was referring to the induced perception on the part of any revolt that "it may be only a regime-sponsored atrocity away from international interveners coming to its aid".[2] This undoubtedly encouraged the Libyans of Benghazi and Assad's opponents in Syria to expect outside intervention if they rose up, leaving the latter feeling betrayed when this did not happen.

Yet Bosnia and Kosovo were highly selective objects of humanitarian ambition. There were many other outrages to which the West turned a blind eye during this time. Despite well-attested atrocities, there were no interventions in Sri Lanka, Sudan, Somalia and Burma. Russia was left a free hand in the Caucasus and Crimea, Indonesia in Aceh and China in Tibet. Ignored too was probably the most blood-thirsty civil war of the age, in Congo, which saw an estimated 3 million war-related deaths.[3] The West's idea of humanitarian was partial, with a peculiar concern for Muslim states.

When attention shifted to Afghanistan and then Iraq quite different motives were in play. Here intervention was a mix of

---

[2] *Guardian Weekly* 10.05.2013.
[3] BBC 20.01.2010.

supposed self-defence, absurd in the case of America and Britain, and punitive regime change. The West simply wanted certain leaders gone and would not be satisfied until this had happened. The reasons seemed almost incidental. As George W. Bush said on one occasion, "law is something I leave to the lawyers".

The catalyst in Afghanistan was the 9/11 attacks by al-Qaeda, but in time this mutated into an ambition to show that the West could rebuild the country's political economy. Bush declared "mission accomplished" in Iraq in a matter of months, but this had to be redefined when the Americans found it impossible to leave. Iraq, like Afghanistan, was to be rebuilt from the bottom up, as envisaged by American neo-conservative think-tanks.

There was no doubting the sincerity with which the "rebuilders" approached their task. There were constant references to "values intervention" and the need for a "paradigm shift" in the countries being occupied. I remember seeing desks lining the walls of the Republican Palace in Iraq, each one labelled with the name of a government department, staffed by eager young officials flown in from Washington. But just as humanitarianism was partial in its application, so was democracy. Dictatorial regimes in Saudi Arabia, the Gulf and central Asia were treated as valued allies.

Confusion over motives played a large part in corrupted implementation. The invading powers, heavily militaristic in character, proved good at regime destroying but not at regime building. Rival defence and diplomatic agencies found it hard to plan strategies for occupation, and thus hard to know when success had been achieved and when it was time to depart. They could not "cut and run". The motto was "The job must be finished", if only to atone for the rising number of war dead.

The methodology of intervention was constantly re-engineered to suit unforeseen crises. It began with rhetorical broadsides, ultimatums and "red lines", followed by economic sanctions and isolation. These tended to induce a siege mentality in the targeted state, strengthening central control, repressing opposition and making a change in policy less rather than more likely. Not one of the sanctions regimes imposed during the period had anything but a counter-productive impact.

The next ratchet of escalation was aerial bombardment. As the historian David Edgerton has pointed out, the extraordinary appeal of air borne weapons to armies down the ages has had little to do with their military effectiveness.[4] There has long been a contrast between the bomb as a tactical aid to ground troops and the "strategic" bombing espoused by Bomber Command's Sir Arthur Harris during World War II. Air forces would constantly overstate their ability to win wars on their own as a way of securing sectional interest.[5] As we have seen, predictions that bombing alone would win in Belgrade, Kabul and Baghdad were unfounded – and rejected by Pentagon analysts.

Throughout the interventions and down to the IS conflict in 2014, politicians would demand air strikes as a sort of "intervention-lite", apparently as a way of expressing their outrage in an appropriately belligerent fashion. Those round David Cameron describe him as fixated on bombing, in Libya, Syria and against IS. Its inaccuracy, destructiveness and counter-productivity when directed at populated areas did nothing to dampen political enthusiasm. Bombing had media impact, and risked no lives on "our" side.

The resulting slaughter of innocents – and the absence of revulsion against it in America and Britain – contrasted with the aversion to infantry atrocities. It was devastating for the West's claims to humanitarianism in the Muslim world. How could the West protest at the carnage of the car and suicide bomber when inflicting similar "collateral damage" from the air. As for the "shock and awe" bombing of Belgrade, Kabul, Baghdad and Tripoli, the phrase itself must qualify as terrorism.

The wars of intervention must be judged by their own ambitions. In former Yugoslavia, the most successful case, Bosnia and Kosovo found their ways into the arms of EU protection through what Knaus rightly called a process of "principled incrementalism, or muddling through with a sense of purpose". At vast cost a shattered nation was

---

[4] Edgerton, *The Shock of the Old: Technology and Global History Since 1990*, 2006.
[5] Neillands, *The Bomber War: Arthur Harris and the Allied Bomber Offensive 1939–45*, 2001.

eventually stabilised and left in peace. The same might be said of the minor example of Sierra Leone. But these were tiny states, two of them smaller than Wales.

Afghanistan was a different matter. The 2001 invasion was a furious, flailing retaliation for 9/11. America's defence secretary, Donald Rumsfeld, was adamant that it was punitive and man-hunting. Capture bin Laden, get out and have no nonsense about nation-building, he said at first. The neo-conservative compulsion to stay and declare "a project" soon overwhelmed such caution.[6] Even so, America handed the job of nation-building, some say cynically, to NATO (and the British). The lessons of that country's history were ignored, including most recently the experience of the Russians in the 1990s. By bolstering the Taliban it spread instability into neighbouring Pakistan, to be exacerbated by the drone war.

Britain's Institute for Strategic Studies concluded in 2010 that the Afghanistan intervention had "ballooned out of all proportion", beyond any conceivable motivation.[7] It concluded that a "long-drawn-out disaster" would lead to inevitable withdrawal that would in time constitute "victory for the enemy". Containment and deterrence would have been a more sensible policy.

In the summer of 2014 Cameron paid probably his last visit to Helmand. The place had cost 453 British soldiers' lives and a staggering £40 billion from the British taxpayer. *The Economist*, which had originally supported the war, commented on the prospect of the Taliban winning, "a great victory ... They will have bled the last vestiges of Britain's claim to global power status into Helmand's sand."[8] Cameron was by then adamant, "We are not going to send combat troops back to Afghanistan."[9]

The motive for Iraq constitutes one of the great puzzles of modern foreign policy. Iraq's possession of a world-threatening arsenal did not wash even at the time. It cannot have been believed by George W. Bush and Tony Blair and, even if true, there was no urgency to resolve

---

[6] Woodward, *Plan of Attack: The Road to War*, 2004.
[7] *Guardian* 08.09.2010.
[8] *The Economist* 11.10.2014.
[9] *Times* 03.10.2014.

it. Yet such was the rush that there was a plan for invasion but none for a subsequent occupation. The dismantling of the Iraqi army in 2003 led swiftly to the rise of Shiʻa and Sunni militias and later to the IS invasion of the north. Far more people died as a result of the collapse of law and order in Iraq than were ever dying before it. It was a parody of a humanitarian intervention. One can only recall Eisenhower's wise advice to his advisers, "Let's make our mistakes slowly." He was the enemy of the "quick fix".

At the time of the invasion, a study by the Carnegie Endowment's Minxin Pei and Sara Kasper pointed out that "historically, nation-building attempts by outside powers are notable mainly for their bitter disappointments, not their triumphs". In 14 cases of American nation-building in underdeveloped societies, Pei and Kasper noted that its aims were achieved only in tiny Panama and Grenada. Worse, "ethnically fragmented countries, such as Iraq, pose extraordinary challenges to nation-builders because, lacking a common national identity, various ethnic groups . . . tend to seize the rare opportunity of outsiders' intervention to seek complete independence or gain more power. This can trigger national disintegration or a backlash from other ethnic groups." This warning was to prove all too relevant in the age of intervention.

Muslims quote the old maxim, better a thousand days of tyranny than one of anarchy. Intervention's collapse of established order in Afghanistan, Iraq and Libya led to anarchy. Despite Blair's 1999 admonition to be prepared for the long haul, forecasts of length of occupation were always fantasy. Britain was to be in Iraq for "less than six months". Bush said the occupation will last "19 months at the very most".[10] In pondering Iraq shortly before his death in 2005, the Cold-War strategist George Kennan, said, "You might start on a war with a purpose . . . but in the end, you find yourself fighting for entirely different things which you had never thought of before." War, he said, "has a momentum of its own . . . You know where you begin. You never know where you are going to end."[11]

---

[10]   Quoted by Lieven, *Times Literary Supplement* 08.05.2013.

[11]   historynewsnetwork.org/article/997#sthash.DRGhGj3J.dpuf.

Iraq has seen no post mortem, audit or explanation, let alone the American remorse and soul-searching that followed Vietnam. As in Afghanistan, the American-led occupation seemed driven by some sense of manifest destiny, an amalgam of a responsibility to protect and a desire to set the world to rights. The yearning for a better planet is not, of itself, an ignoble one and has sometimes rescued the community nations from appalling horrors. But yearning and achieving are not the same.

I asked at the start, whether there were deeper forces at work, impelling the Western democracies through the age of intervention. Though it was heavily biased towards the Muslim world, I never subscribed to the view that it was driven by oil, religion or some regional strategic imperative, much as Blair's rhetoric sometimes suggested otherwise. As the wars were prolonged, conspiracy theorists had a field day, but while conspiracy has some part to play in history, it is usually an incidental part. As Tuchman wrote, folly not conspiracy is a far more prominent actor.[12]

I am less dismissive of the latent neo-imperialism that still runs strong in the veins of NATO leaders and their military establishments. It could be remarkably explicit. In 2002 the British diplomat and Blair adviser, Robert Cooper, gave what became a clarion call for intervention. He declared "a new kind of imperialism, one acceptable to a world of human rights and cosmopolitan values ... which like all imperialism aims to bring order and organisation but which rests today on the voluntary principle".[13]

Cooper glossed over so many questions – what is acceptable, what is order, what is voluntary – as to be helpless as a guide to policy. But his words sanctified the interventionist cause and cleansed it of the charge of cynical imperialism. When publicity for atrocities demanded that "something be done", humanitarian intervention was a concept to hand. Post-modern world powers, to Cooper, were exonerated from the UN Charter's original respect for national sovereignty. As if by virtue of their triumph in the Cold War, the

---

[12] Barbara Tuchman, *The March of Folly*, 1984.
[13] *Observer* 07.04.2002.

Americans in particular regarded themselves as moral arbiters of their own actions.

Nor can we discount the ambition, perhaps self-delusion, of the leaders themselves. It was certainly clear to those round him that Blair, like many British leaders before and since, craved a role on the world stage. Shortly after taking office he bemoaned to his aide, Alastair Campbell, that "Britain is such a small country", prompting Campbell to wonder sardonically if they might seize some other European country to become bigger.[14] After 9/11 his utterances took on a near messianic streak. He told the Chilcot Inquiry into the Iraq War that he took pride in toppling dictators, in making the world "safe for democracy". Blair's foreign policy often seemed a throwback to Kipling's Empire, where, "a court-house stands where the regiment go-ed. And the river's clean where the raw blood flowed."

I am sure one reason for the lack of post mortem is the fact of a wide left-right consensus in favour of intervention. America was able to call on a remarkable range of allies to launder its various invasions in the eyes of the world. Twenty-eight states supported NATO's Operation Enduring Freedom in 2001 in Afghanistan, including many that were not even NATO members. Forty states rallied to America's summons of a "coalition of the willing" against Iraq in 2003. They came from as far afield as Tonga, Iceland, Mongolia and Honduras, though most had gone within three years. A dozen nations even signed up to bombing IS in 2014.

Neo-conservatives and liberals found different but equally powerful reasons for reordering the post-Cold War world. It was remarkable that in almost every case – until the IS invasion – war was waged by the West on the side of rebellion against an established regime. Western armies were to spend two decades abetting insurgency, separatism, religious extremism and instability. The age of intervention was no age of conservatism but rather an age of revolution. At times its fervid apologias wavered between the medieval crusades and the outpourings of the Soviet Comintern.

---

[14] Alastair Campbell, *Diaries*.

To this the American Cato Institute retorted with properly conservative scepticism. Its Iraq reports from 2003 onwards noted "a worrisome consensus emerging among humanitarian hawks on the left and neo-conservatives on the right", always in favour of intervention. As motives coalesced round "the War on Terror", Cato warned against exaggerating the power of al-Qaeda and others that posed no "existential" threat to any Western country. As for nation-building missions, they were "extremely costly, most of them fail and most corrode American power". At the time this was spitting in the wind.

I doubt if these disparate motives are ever to be resolved. They emanate not from a humanitarian imperative. This has shown itself vulnerable to selective application and often non-humanitarian implementation. It has at best short-term relevance. The age of intervention suffered instead from the arrogance that power grants to leaders of nations and the interests, lobbies and public opinion that swirl round them. It saw in all its pomp what Eisenhower warned was an emerging "military-industrial" complex that risked taking decision out of the hands of democracy. I regard that risk as never higher than today.

Power confers its own moral superiority. Even so cautious a statesman as Bush's secretary of state, Colin Powell, could find himself declaring that "every country is touched by America ... It has an interest in every place on this Earth. We need to lead, to guide, to help in every country that has a desire to be free, open, and prosperous."[15] Such high-flown sentiments easily elide into imperial self-righteousness and self-delusion, impelled onwards by the magnet of military glory. No democratic politician is immune to such inducements.

The danger in this craving is that it needs constant sustenance. In Britain Cameron had hardly ended one intervention before he was searching for another. These gained public support in the aggressor countries through politicians exploiting fear, fear of attack, fear of foreigners, fear of religious extremism. The implausible risk posed by

---

[15] Senate hearings 17.01.2001.

terrorism to "national security" was a running theme of every speech by Bush after 9/11. It is still a leitmotif of pronouncements by American and British leaders.

The crucial bellwether throughout this period was American public opinion, tentative at first, militant after 9/11, then increasingly exhausted. It was driven by what the RAND Corporation, in its *Beginner's Guide to Nation Building* (2007), described as an assumption that after the Cold War America could do anything "through a well-considered application of personnel and money, over extended periods of time". In the new century, said RAND, America would have the power to end atrocities, overthrow dictators, rebuild nations and create global democracy.

Such grandiose ambition required grandiose enemies. American propagandists of the War on Terror brought to mind the dismay of Senator Kefauver's investigation into organised crime in the 1950s, which found time and again that it was dealing with small-time crooks rather than a grand and sinister international mafia. The New York academic, David Harvey, found reasons for the Iraq War lying close to home. He quoted Hannah Arendt's account of "the long history of governments in trouble seeking to solve their problems either by foreign adventures or by manufacturing foreign threats to consolidate solidarities at home".[16] The politics of fear may be as old as the hills. But it is regularly refreshed by modern democratic leaders. Alarming intelligence, an occasional atrocity and a compliant media all served to generate alarm in the cause of intervention.

Such manipulation of popular sentiment can be taken too far. Though they were supported by successive American and British leaders, the wars of intervention were to prove the most controversial since Vietnam. Not only did Russia, China, much of Asia and Latin America stand aloof, but the fact that victim states were overwhelmingly Muslim caused painful divisions in countries with large Muslim populations. A widespread accusation was that so-called "liberal intervention" was merely a cloak for bombastic imperialism. On 15 February 2003 with the invasion of

---

[16] Harvey, *The New Imperialism*, 2003.

Iraq looming, there were demonstrations in 600 world cities against it. They involved from six to ten million people, rated the largest mass protest in history.

This scepticism never went away. In August 2013 Cameron was rebuffed by Britain's House of Commons on his wish to intervene militarily in the Syrian civil war. In private meetings, he was reportedly frantic for bombing, eager to repeat what he saw as his success in Libya. Though his advisers argued the absence of any tactical endgame, let alone a strategic plan, it was the Commons that reflected public opinion and forced Cameron to back down. His alarmist rhetoric – that Syria posed "a direct threat to this country" – was so implausible it had lost its capacity to scare.

Among the many casualties of the age of intervention was the United Nations. Once the supposed arbiter of global law and order, its influence declined to near nothing. Previous operations in Congo, Cyprus, Lebanon and Bosnia had seen "blue berets" in the ascendant, policing contested borders and overseeing refugee movements. Now the UN was handicapped by Russian vetoes. Its early failure to curb violence in Bosnia collapsed faith in its authority. But while America mostly ignored the UN, its legal imprimatur was still crucial for retaining wide support for its actions. In Libya great ingenuity went into the wording of resolutions to support aggression.

The reality of the age of intervention is that it was intellectually incoherent. At its start, Europe had fallen out of love with war, or at least out of practice. Its most astute historian, Michael Howard, could discourse in 2000 on the passing of the "keen young specialists in violence ... who were classless, efficient, and above all enjoyed fighting". They had been replaced by "ritualised nuclear threats" and the advent of high-tech stand-off weaponry. To Howard, Europe had become pacified, "debellicised".[17]

This judgment proved premature. Over the next 15 years, the zest for wars of intervention left an estimated 250,000 people dead, few of whom had any quarrel with the West. It left many more maimed, tortured, impoverished and driven into exile. The world is

---

[17] Howard, *The Invention of Peace*, 2000.

not safer or happier as a result, rather it is more distressed and dangerous. The wars did not invalidate all forms of intervention, indeed it would be an added condemnation of them if it did. Humanity continues to demand our eyes and ears, and sometimes our fighting spirit. I would redouble any effort to dispense relief to the victims of any conflict. I would accept that, just occasionally (as in Kosovo), violence is the lesser of evils.

The most thorough account of "The 9/11 Wars", by the journalist Jason Burke, portrays them in essence not as a cosmic struggle between the West and militant Islam, as presented by Bush and Blair, but rather as a kaleidoscope of local disputes into which the West intruded in variously ham-fisted fashion.[18] The West's eventual retreat left no winners or losers. Certainly bin Laden's al-Qaeda had not persuaded south-east Asia to rise up in unison against the evil empire of the West. But nor had the "neo-con crusade" delivered a peaceful and prosperous zone of pro-Western regimes. The legacy, says Burke, is of a "socially conservative, moderately Islamist, strongly nationalist narrative that ... will pose an increasingly coherent challenge to the ability of America and European nations to pursue their interests on a global stage".

As conflicts in the region were "re-localised" – in Syria, Iraq, Libya and Yemen – the detritus of conflict continued to litter the theatre of intervention. The retreat of Western armies was covered by regular drone assaults, as if to remind the Muslim world of the West's awesome if waning potency. Order lay in ruins and chaos asserted its dominance. Millions of refugees were uprooted and cultural artefacts were destroyed. But the War on Terror busied itself elsewhere, worrying over how to de-radicalise Muslim youths in Western countries, and how to assimilate waves of asylum seekers. Besides, Russia was flexing its muscles. Foreign policy could revert to familiar territory.

It is hard to look back over the period without a sense of historical repetition. In 1997 the Gandhian expert, Bhikhu Perekh, wrote a lengthy critique of what was to prove the prevailing ideology of the

---

[18] Burke, *The 9/11 Wars*, 2012.

age. Humanitarian intervention, he said, should be distinguished from charitable aid. It tended to war, and war in a humanitarian cause was a concept "inherently incapable of carrying the burden of hope placed on it". It was therefore in danger of becoming "a grand moral spectacle in which the heroic, Christian West yet again asserts its moral superiority and reinforces racist stereotypes traditionally used to justify colonialism".[19]

I am normally averse to such neo-imperialist analysis of contemporary conflicts. Here I find it hard to disagree with Perekh's prophecy. The philanthropic motives claimed for these wars were bogus, overwhelmed by the politics of fear in Western democracies and by the military/industrial juggernauts of Western armies on the warpath.

For the West these were wars of choice, but for their victims they were wars of compulsion. Their philanthropy proved a snare and a delusion, mocking the liberties in whose name they were fought. The armed clash of states remains the most primitive and intractable of human events. The eternal quest continues to render them defunct.

---

[19] West, "Rethinking Humanitarian Intervention", *International Political Science Review*.

Bibliography

Blix, Hans, *Disarming Iraq* (London: Bloomsbury, 2005).

Burke, Jason, *Al-Qaeda: The True Story of Radical Islam* (London: Penguin, 2007).

———, *The 9/11 Wars* (London: Penguin, 2012).

Campbell, Alastair, *The Alastair Campbell Diaries, Volume One* (London: Random House, 2010).

Clarke, Richard A., *Against All Enemies: Inside America's War on Terror* (New York, NY: Free Press, 2004).

Cooper, Robert, *The Breaking of Nations: Order and Chaos in the Twenty-First Century* (London: Atlantic Books, 2003).

Cowper-Coles, Sherard, *Cables from Kabul: The Inside Story of West Afghanistan's Campaign* (London: HarperPress, 2011).

Dean, John W., *Worse than Watergate: The Secret Presidency of George W. Bush* (New York, NY: Little, Brown and Company, 2004).

Dobbins, James, Jones, Seth G., Crane, Keith and Cole DeGrasse, Beth, *The Beginner's Guide to Nation-Building* (Santa Monica, CA: RAND Corporation, 2007).

Dobbins, James, Jones, Seth G., Crane, Keith and Cole DeGrasse, Beth, *The Beginner's Guide to Nation Building* (Pittsburgh: RAND Corporation, 2007).

Edgerton, David, *The Shock of the Old: Technology and Global History Since 1900* (London: Profile Books, 2006).

Goldstein, Gordon, *Lessons in Disaster: McGeorge Bundy and the Path to War in Vietnam* (New York, NY: Times Books, 2008).

Haidt, Jonathan, *The Righteous Mind: Why Good People Are Divided By Politics* (New York, NY: Pantheon Books, 2012).

Harvey, David, *The New Imperialism* (Oxford: Oxford University Press, 2003).

Healy, Gene, "The Iraq War was a Bipartisan Disaster" (Washington: Cato Institute, 2014).

Howard, Michael, *The Invention of Peace: Reflections on War and International Order* (London: Profile Books, 2000).

Howard, Roger, *What's Wrong with Liberal Interventionism: The Dangers and Delusions of Interventionist Doctrine* (London: Social Affairs Unit, 2006).

Kampfner, John, *Blair's Wars* (New York, NY: Free Press, 2003).

Neillands, Robin, *The Bomber War: Arthur Harris and the Allied Bomber Offensive 1939–45* (London: John Murray, 2001).

Nye, Joseph, *Soft Power: The Means to Success in World Politics* (New York, NY: PublicAffairs, 2004).

Oborne, Peter, *The Use and Abuse of Terror: The Construction of a False Narrative on the Domestic Terror Threat* (London: Centre for Policy Studies, 2006).

Owen, David, *Balkan Odyssey* (London: Weidenfeld and Nicolson, 1995).

Pei, Minxin and Kasper Sara, "Lessons from the Past: The American Record on Nation Building" (Washington: Carnegie Endowment for International Peace), 2003.

Perry, Mark, *How to Lose the War on Terror* (London: C. Hurst & Co Publishers, 2010).

Prados, John, *Hoodwinked: The Documents That Reveal How Bush Sold Us a War* (New York, NY: The New Press, 2004).

Ricks, Thomas E., *Fiasco: The American Military Adventure in Iraq* (London: Allen Lane, 2006).

Rifkind, Gabrielle and Giandomenico Picco, *The Fog of Peace: The Human Face of Conflict Resolution* (London: I.B.Tauris, 2014).

Ross, Carne, *The Leaderless Revolution: How Ordinary People Can Take Power and Change Politics in the Twenty-First Century* (New York, NY: Simon & Schuster, 2011).

Runciman, David, *The Politics of Good Intentions: History, Fear and Hypocrisy in the New World Order* (Princeton, NJ: Princeton University Press, 2006).

Schell, Jonathan, *The Unconquerable World: Power, Nonviolence, and the Will of the People* (New York, NY: Metropolitan Books, 2003).

Smith, Rupert, *The Utility of Force: The Art of War in the Modern World* (London: Penguin, 2006).

Sorley, Lewis, *A Better War: the Unexamined Victories and the Final Tragedy of America's Last Years in Vietnam* (San Diego, CA: Harcourt Brace International, 1999).

Stewart, Rory and Knaus, Gerald, *Can Intervention Work?* (New York: W.W. Norton & Company, 2011).

Stiglitz, Joseph and Bilmes, Linda, *The Trillion Dollar War: The True Cost of the Iraq Conflict* (London: Allen Lane, 2008).

Suskind, Ron, *The Price of Loyalty: George W. Bush, the White House, and the Education of Paul O'Neill* (New York, NY: Simon & Schuster, 2004).

Synnott, Hilary, *Bad Days in Basra: My Turbulent Time as Britain's Man in Southern Iraq* (London: I.B.Tauris, 2008).

Tuchman, Barbara, *The March of Folly: From Troy to Vietnam* (New York, NY: Alfred A. Knopf, 1984).

Wills, Gary, *Bomb Power: The Modern Presidency and the National Security State* (London: Penguin, 2010).

Wilson, Joseph, *The Politics of Truth: Inside the Lies That Led to War and Betrayed My Wife's CIA Identity* (New York, NY: Carroll & Graf, 2004).

Woodward, Bob, *Plan of Attack: The Road to War* (New York, NY: Simon & Schuster, 2004).

Wright, Lawrence, *The Looming Tower: Al-Qaeda and the Road to 9/11* (New York, NY: Alfred A. Knopf, 2006).

Index